FISH FOR TODAY

JOHN WEST

HAMLYN

CONTENTS

- All calorie values are approximate
- Microwave information is for a 650 watt oven

Photography by David Jordan
Decorative illustrations by Jane Brewster
Step-by-step illustrations by Sandra Pond

Published by
The Hamlyn Publishing Group Limited,
Bridge House, 69 London Road, Twickenham,
Middlesex, England.

First published 1987

ISBN 0 600 55411 2

Set in Monophoto Gill Sans by Servis Filmsetting Ltd, Manchester
Printed in Spain

THE JOHN WEST STORY

John West Foods is one of the world's leading canned food companies with a reputation for providing a wide range of canned goods of the very highest quality.

But think of John West and the chances are you will think of canned salmon – the association goes back many years, to 1861 in fact, when two Liverpool merchants, Pelling and Stanley, formed a 'Provisions, Fruit and Canned Goods Business' at a time when canned food was in the early stages of development.

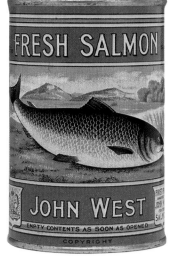

The introduction of canned salmon to this country was born as much from the social and economic needs of the Industrial Revolution as it was from sheer commercial enterprise. Pelling and Stanley were quick to recognise the need for easily transportable, high-protein food for the industrial workers of the north – and what better than canned salmon? It was from John West, a Scotsman who had opened the first salmon cannery in Westport, Oregon in 1857, that they purchased their first consignment. Trade flourished and Pelling and Stanley purchased the rights to the now famous John West brand.

Little did these founding fathers realise that they were sowing the seeds of a truly international company that was to set the standards in canned foods for the years to come, with a range now spanning not only the traditional John West Salmon and 'Skippers' brands but other canned fish, fruit, vegetables and meat.

Today, with over 120 years experience in canned food, John West is one of the strongest brand names in the world, a brand synonymous with quality.

JOHN WEST - INSIST ON THE BEST

In an ever demanding world, John West quality standards have become even more stringent – indeed they are the very cornerstone of the John West business. Buyers travel the world searching for and demanding the highest quality available – bringing salmon, tuna, fruit and meat from wherever the best is to be found.

Our insistence on the best does not stop there. Quality control continues at our headquarters in Liverpool, where products are meticulously checked for safety and can contents are examined for quality of appearance, flavour, colour and texture. These quality and safety standards are consistent right across the John West range, hence the now legendary advertising line coined in the phrase 'It's the fish John West reject that makes John West the best'.

Why canned fish?

Over the last few years, we have all noticed a change in the way we live our lives today. Increased pressure on our time has led us to rely much more on convenience foods and appliances, such as microwave ovens. The healthy eating trend has encouraged us to adopt a more balanced approach to our diets and an ever increasing array of foodstuffs on supermarket shelves has made us even more discerning in terms of the choice, quality and taste appeal of the food we buy.

Canned fish has been around for many years, but it is perhaps more relevant to today's lifestyle than ever before. All fish and seafoods share the advantages of being healthy foods, providing nutritional essentials, flavour and variety – but to these qualities, canning adds convenience.

The very nature of the canning process ensures that a product's natural freshness is maintained. Only the finest fish are selected by John West – they are then canned and cooked to ensure that all the flavour and goodness remains safely locked in.

Canned fish for health

With today's increased awareness of the link between diet and health we are all paying much more attention to the type of food we eat, checking that it contains essential nutrients and exercising caution perhaps where products contain unnecessary additives.

John West canned fish is natural and traditional favourites such as salmon, tuna, pilchards and sardines are free from any artificial additives. All ingredients are declared on the label so that you know exactly what you are buying.

Few foods make as valuable a contribution to a healthy diet as canned fish. It is a natural and valuable source of protein, containing amino acids vital for growth and repair of body cells and tissue. It contains essential vitamins to help us fight infection and maintain normal metabolism and body growth. Canned fish also contains an appreciable quantity of minerals which assist the development of healthy bones and teeth, particularly important for children.

We should all be aware of the danger of eating too much saturated fat – the type found in red meats and dairy products for example. The fat present in canned fish, and the oil in which it is packed, is polyunsaturated and broadly considered to be beneficial to our health since it does not increase the level of cholesterol in our blood. Research suggests that this may help to prevent heart disease.

Canned fish is a natural choice if we are pursuing a healthier diet and if we are looking to reduce our calorie intake, then canned fish in brine is ideal. For example a 100 g/4 oz serving of tuna in oil contains 197 calories compared with tuna in brine which contains only 110 calories.

There is now an extensive range of canned fish in brine, not only tuna but also sardines, pilchards, mackerel, shrimps and prawns.

Canned fish for convenience

You should never be without a good supply of canned fish because when those unexpected guests call or the children 'whiz in', looking for a quick snack, canned fish is ready in an instant – no waste, no messy preparation. Whether you want to make something quick and simple in minutes – or spend a little more time to create something special – canned fish is versatile and reliable.

Canned fish for variety

With a can of fish you need never be short of inspiration and ideas. The range is now extensive with a choice of fish canned in oil, tomato, brine and savoury sauces – so there is something to suit all tastes.

FISH FACTS

Fish are almost numberless in their variety and many are now available canned. Here is some information on the most popular varieties.

Anchovies Anchovies are fished from spring through to summer. Before canning, they are filleted, salted, then packed in oil which gives them a deliciously strong flavour – hence a little anchovy goes a long way!

Brisling The first smoked brisling was produced in very small quantities in 1879 but it was in fact 1889 before the product found its way into the UK.

Sold under the famous John West 'Skippers' brand, brisling are members of the herring family and are also known as sprats. These tasty little fish have a lightly smoked flavour and are canned in oil or tomato sauce. Each can of John West 'Skippers' has at least eight fish.

Pressed Cod Roe Cod is fished within the Arctic Circle and the Baltic Sea. The roe is removed from the female fish aboard the vessel at sea, and stored in chilled crates. There are various qualities of roe, but only the finest goes into the cans for John West. During the canning process the roe is mixed with flour to form the finished product.

Soft Cod Roe/Soft Herring Roe This product is from the male of each species and again it is taken from the fish at sea. Roe is difficult to handle and it must be canned within hours of landing.

Crab The traditional King and Queen Crab are caught in cold waters, for example around the coast of Canada. These species of crab are in limited supply in canned form but the UK market has been increasingly supplied with white meat crab from warm waters, particularly Thailand.

Dressed Crab This spread is prepared from local crab caught in the coastal waters of the UK and Norway. After cooking, the crab meat is ground to a spreading consistency, seasoned and canned. John West dressed crab contains 93% crabmeat.

Herrings The word 'herring' means 'army' and describes the large shoals in which these fish swim around the waters of the British Isles and Canada. Herrings are small fish with a delicate flavour. The bones are removed before the fish are canned in tomato or savoury sauce.

Kippers Kippers are smoked herrings. Once caught, the herrings are filleted and naturally smoked to give them their own distinctive flavour, then canned in vegetable oil.

The great appeal of canned kippers is that you enjoy the full flavour of traditional kippers, with neither the messy preparation nor the bones and lingering smells. To serve them hot simply place the unopened can in boiling water for 7 minutes.

Mackerel A long slender fish with a firm flesh that has a sharp positive flavour all of its own. Mackerel is caught in the waters around the British Isles and it is canned at the peak of freshness. Mackerel is available in steak or fillet form, in oil, brine or tomato sauce. It is also available smoked.

Pilchards Pilchards can be found all over the world, from the Cornish coast to as far away as South America and Japan. They are similar to a sardine but larger in size, and are renowned for being superbly nutritious and excellent value.

Salmon 'The King of Fish' as it is often known, salmon is prized worldwide as a delectable food.

Nature restricts the range of salmon, by water temperature, to the sea and cold mountain streams. Despite the fact that the salmon spends the greater part of its life out at sea, its dependance on freshwater, for breeding and the survival of its young, is absolute. And so, when the salmon is ready to spawn, it leaves the ocean and returns to the exact waters of its birth.

This is truly a remarkable feat, for the salmon must ascend swift mountain rivers and pass over waterfalls and obstacles during its upstream migration. It is from this astonishing ability that the salmon derives its name, taken from the Latin word 'Salmo' meaning 'leaper'. The following four main varieties of Pacific Salmon are used in canning.

Red or Sockeye Salmon - The prize of the catch – this fish weighs around 4 to 12 pounds and is a deep natural red in colour, with a firm texture and a rich flavour. More expensive than other canned salmon varieties, but worth it for a special treat.

Medium Red or Coho Salmon is slightly less red, has large flakes and a fine flavour.

Pink Salmon is the smallest of Pacific salmon averaging about 4 pounds. It is somewhat softer than other species, contains very little oil and has a light, delicate flavour. Pink Salmon is a versatile ingredient for use in hot dishes and it provides an economical way of enjoying the great taste of salmon every day.

Keta Salmon is lighter in colour and has less oil than other varieties. This fish is particularly good for slimmers.

Sardines   Sardines were the first variety of fish to be canned back in 1822 in France and the name originated from the Island of Sardinia. Today, vast quantities of these fish are caught off the coasts of Spain, Italy, Portugal, Yugoslavia and North Africa.

Shrimps and Prawns   These prolific crustaceans are fished in almost every part of the world and hundreds of different species have been recorded. They are highly prized as a delicious, nutritrious seafood and they are good as part of a healthy diet as they contain little fat and provide plenty of protein. Shrimps and prawns develop their natural pink colour when cooked before canning.

Sild   This fish derives its name from the Norwegian word meaning 'small herring'. Today sild are found around the coasts of the British Isles and Norway. Sild have a distinctive, mild flavour and they are canned in oil or tomato sauce.

Smoked Mussels, Oysters and Baby Clams   As our interest in seafood generally has increased over the last few years, so these delicately flavoured shellfish have gained in popularity. Canned shellfish are convenient (no need for messy shelling) and versatile in hors d'oeuvres and canapés or for adding that extra flavour to soups and other dishes.

Tuna   Tuna has been considered a delicacy for hundreds of years. Vase paintings on the famous red and black pottery produced in ancient Greece show tuna being prepared for the tables of the epicureans and tunny, as it is still called in the Mediterranean, was a favourite food in Rome in the great days of the Roman Empire.

Tuna was first canned in 1903 in Los Angeles and rapidly became an important food during the First World War, when many foods became scarce. John West pioneered canned tuna in Britain over thirty years ago and today it represents the most popular variety of canned fish, both here and around the world.

Tuna is a generic name describing a large number of species of which skipjack and yellowfin are the most commonly used in canning. Skipjack tuna is light tan in colour with pinkish overtones, a soft texture and a full flavour. Yellowfin tuna is lighter in colour with a finer texture and a more delicate taste. Tuna is fished throughout a wide area of the tropics and sub-tropics, embracing the south west coast of America, the western reaches of the Central and South Pacific up to Japan, the Indian Ocean and west along the equator, from Africa to South America.

The John West canned tuna range now caters for all purposes and preferences and comprises steaks, chunks and sandwich tuna, all canned in oil or brine. Also available is an exciting range of tuna in sauces, including tuna in mayonnaise with sweetcorn, tuna in curry sauce, tuna in barbecue sauce and tuna in tomato sauce. They can be used in salads or as a delicious filling for baked potatoes, quiches, vols-au-vent, stuffed peppers, avocados or a variety of other dishes.

Storage and Handling of Canned Fish

- Canned fish has a long shelf life. However, there are certain storage periods which should not be exceeded if you wish to enjoy the fish at its best:

  canned fish in oil – up to 5 years
  (anchovies up to 2 years)
  canned fish in sauce – up to 2 years
  canned fish in brine – up to 5 years

  This does not mean that after the periods mentioned above the fish would be bad or unsafe but it may not be at its best.

- Cans should be stored in a cool, dry place. High temperature can spoil the flavour and colour, whilst storage under damp conditions can lead to rust, holing and decomposition.

- Never use a can that is leaking or blown. You will recognise a blown can because the ends will bulge outwards.

- Avoid badly dented cans, particularly if they are dented near the seams.

- Once a can is opened transfer any unused contents to a dish, cover and refrigerate. It is worth remembering that once a can has been opened the food in it will only keep as long as fresh food which has been similarly cooked.

SNACK-ATTACK

Snacks are very much a part of our everyday diets but they can lack imagination. So, next time you feel a snack-attack coming on, quickly look through these pages and you will find lots of tempting recipes.

Canned fish is ideal for a quick snack because it is ready to serve straight from the can and full of natural goodness. Apart from being an obvious sandwich food or toast-topper, canned fish can also be transformed into a variety of tempting snacks.

These speedy recipes can all be prepared in 15 minutes so you will not be overcome with hunger pangs before your snack is ready to eat. They all taste so good that you may well decide to offer some of the recipes as first courses too.

KIPPER RAREBIT

SERVES 4

390 Kcals per portion

Here is a delicious variation on that old favourite, Welsh rarebit. As well as making an excellent snack, this recipe goes down just as well as a first course – cut the slices into triangles and overlap them on individual plates to look attractive.

15 g/½ oz butter or margarine
15 g/½ oz flour
200 g/7 oz Cheddar cheese, grated
250 ml/8 fl oz flat beer
1 teaspoon mustard powder
pinch of cayenne
1 (200-g) can kipper fillets, drained and flaked
salt and pepper
4 slices wholemeal bread, toasted
lemon wedges · parsley sprigs

Put the butter or margarine, flour, cheese, beer, mustard powder and cayenne in a saucepan and stir over a low heat until the mixture is smooth. Stir in the kippers and check the seasoning. Simmer for 2–3 minutes.

Spread the mixture evenly over the slices of toast and place under the grill until brown and bubbling. Garnish each rarebit with a lemon wedge and parsley sprig.

◆ MICRO-TIP

The rarebit mixture can be cooked in a large basin in the microwave. Put the flour and mustard in the basin, then whisk in the beer. Cook on high for 3 minutes. Whisk well, then beat in remaining ingredients. Cook on high for a further 3–4 minutes, beating well halfway through. The mixture should be smooth and thick. Spread on toast and grill as above.

QUICK PORTUGUESE PIZZA

SERVES 4

150 Kcals per portion

Sliced processed cheese is a good standby for speedy snacks but if you have a few seconds to spare, try using some sliced Mozzarella cheese instead.

2 muffins or baps, split
tomato ketchup
1 (120-g) can sardines in oil, drained
4 slices processed cheese
dried oregano
black olives

Spread the cut surfaces of the muffins or baps with tomato ketchup. Put a sardine on top of each and cover with a cheese slice. Brush with a little of the sardine oil, sprinkle with oregano and garnish with olives. Place under a moderate grill for 10 minutes, or in a moderately hot oven (200 C, 400 F, gas 6) for 10 minutes.

COOK'S TIP

Savoury butters can be made using various canned fish. Remember you can always make these 'butters' with polyunsaturated margarine. Try some of the following ideas – remember you can always freeze any leftover butter. Spread the butters on hot toast, on to slices of French bread to heat in the oven or on plain crackers.

Anchovy Butter
Mash 1 (50-g) can anchovies with the oil and beat into 75 g/3 oz softened butter adding a little freshly ground black pepper and a dash of lemon juice.

Sardine Butter
Mash 1 (120-g) can sardines with the grated rind of 1 lemon and a squeeze of lemon juice. Add seasoning to taste, then gradually beat into 100 g/4 oz softened butter.

Shrimp Butter
Drain 1 (100-g) can shrimps and chop finely. Beat into 75 g/3 oz softened butter, adding seasoning, a dash of lemon juice and 2 tablespoons chopped parsley.

PIZZA TOASTS

SERVES 2

235 Kcals per portion

These tempting pizza-style snacks really are delicious and satisfying. If you enjoy full-flavoured foods you may like to add a small crushed garlic clove and a pinch of dried mixed herbs to the skippers.

2 slices wholemeal bread
1 (106-g) can skippers in tomato sauce, flaked
50 g/2 oz Cheddar cheese, grated
1 tomato, thinly sliced

Toast one side of the bread. Spread the flaked skippers over the untoasted side of the bread. Sprinkle the cheese on top and garnish with the tomato. Place under a moderate grill for 5 minutes, or until golden and bubbling. Serve immediately.

EGG RAMEKINS

SERVES 4

310 Kcals per portion

25 g/1 oz butter
4 eggs
4 tablespoons milk or single cream
1 (50-g) can anchovies, drained
50 g/2 oz Cheshire, Lancashire or Caerphilly cheese, crumbled

Heat the oven to moderately hot (200 C, 400 F, gas 6). Use the butter to thoroughly grease four ramekin dishes. Crack an egg into each and add a tablespoon of milk or cream. Top each with crossed anchovies and a little cheese.

Stand the ramekins on a baking tray and bake for 10–12 minutes, or until the eggs are just set. Serve at once with hot toast or bread and butter.

SALMON SNACKS

SERVES 4

280 Kcals per portion

| 1 (213-g) can pink salmon, drained and flaked |
| 100 g / 4 oz fresh breadcrumbs |
| 2 celery sticks, finely chopped |
| 2 spring onions, finely chopped |
| 1 egg, beaten |
| salt and pepper |
| oil for frying |
| 2 muffins or baps, split and toasted |
| mayonnaise |

Combine the salmon with the breadcrumbs, celery, onions, egg and seasoning. Mix well and form into four cakes on a floured board.

Fry in hot oil for 5 minutes, turning once, or until golden. Place a salmon cake on each muffin or bap half and serve with a little mayonnaise and salad.

ANCHOVY AND EGG SPREAD

SERVES 4

300 Kcals per portion

This tasty spread is delicious on toasts or split French bread or rolls or with crackers.

| 4 hard-boiled eggs |
| 1 (50-g) can anchovies |
| 100 g / 4 oz cream cheese or low fat soft cheese |
| freshly ground black pepper |
| 2 teaspoons lemon juice |
| 2 tablespoons chopped chives or parsley |
| Garnish (optional) |
| sliced hard-boiled egg |
| anchovy fillets |

Thoroughly mash the eggs, then add the anchovies with the oil from the can and mash them with the eggs. Mix with the soft cheese, pepper and lemon. Beat in the chives or parsley. Garnish, if you like.

FRENCH SARDINE TOASTS

SERVES 4

235 Kcals per portion

Cayenne is a fiery hot pepper that can be used to add zest to recipes such as this one but do take care not to add too much of this seasoning!

100 g/4 oz Cheddar cheese, grated
1 teaspoon prepared mustard
pinch of cayenne
1 (120-g) can sardines in oil, drained and flaked
4 pieces French bread, split lengthways

Put the cheese, mustard and cayenne in a saucepan and mix together. Add the sardines and heat gently for 2–3 minutes. Spread the mixture over the pieces of French bread and place under a moderate grill until browned.

Variations Canned mackerel in brine or smoked mackerel also taste good in this recipe. You can add additional topping ingredients once the fish is grilled; for example try some of the following ideas.
Tomatoes and Olives: Stone and halve 50 g/2 oz black or green olives, then mix with 3 chopped tomatoes and 1 tablespoon chopped parsley.
Cucumber and Spring Onion: Top each piece with a few slices of cucumber and a little chopped spring onion.
Paprika Eggs: Chop hard-boiled eggs and arrange on the toasts. Sprinkle with a little paprika.
Apple and Spring Onion: (particularly good with smoked mackerel) Core and slice 1 or 2 dessert apples, arrange on toasts and sprinkle with a little chopped spring onion.

COOK'S TIP

If the oil from a can of fish is not required in the recipe, then it can be used to make a full-flavoured dressing for salad to serve with the dish.

TUNA OMELETTES

SERVES 4

330 Kcals per portion

Fill a plain omelette with a creamy tuna mixture to make an interesting snack. You can use snipped chives instead of the spring onions and add a little grated lemon rind – delicious!

1 (185-g) can tuna chunks in brine, drained and flaked
4 spring onions, trimmed and chopped
salt and pepper
4 tablespoons soured cream or mayonnaise
8 eggs
about 150 ml/$\frac{1}{4}$ pint milk
50 g/2 oz butter or 4 tablespoons oil for cooking

Mix the tuna with the spring onions and seasoning to taste, then stir in the soured cream or mayonnaise.

Beat 2 eggs thoroughly until really frothy, then beat in a little seasoning and 2 tablespoons of the milk. Melt a quarter of the butter, or heat 1 tablespoon oil, in an omelette pan and roll the pan to coat the base evenly with fat. When really hot, pour in the eggs and cook over a fairly high heat until beginning to set. Lift the edges of the omelette to let any unset egg run on to the hot surface of the pan.

When bubbling and browned underneath, quickly spread about a quarter of the filling on one side of the omelette and fold the other half over. Slide the omelette out on to a warmed plate and serve immediately. Cook the other omelettes in the same way.

A Variety of Omelette Fillings

Salmon and Sweetcorn
Drain and flake 1 (213-g) can pink salmon. Mix with 1 (326-g) can sweetcorn (drained), 4 tablespoons mayonnaise and seasoning to taste.

Herrings and Spring Onion
Drain and flake 1 (200-g) can herring fillets. Mix with 6 chopped spring onions, seasoning to taste and 4 tablespoons soured cream.

Anchovy and Tomato
Peel and chop 8 tomatoes. Chop 1 (50-g) can anchovies and add to the tomatoes with the oil from the can. Stir in plenty of chopped parsley and freshly ground black pepper.

Anchovies with Cottage Cheese
Drain and chop 1 (50-g) can anchovies then add to 350 g/12 oz cottage cheese. Mix in 2 tablespoons chopped chives and freshly ground black pepper.

Crab and Courgette
Trim 4 small courgettes and cut into chunks. Sauté briefly in a knob of butter, then mix with (170-g) can white meat crab and seasoning to taste. Set aside to fill the omelettes.

Spicy Pilchard and Tomato
Flake 1 (215-g) can pilchards in tomato sauce and add 2 teaspoons ground coriander. Add a pinch of ground ginger and seasoning to taste.

COOK'S TIP

The best way to cut chives is to hold the bunch firmly and snip off the ends with a pair of clean scissors.

MACKEREL SMALTZ STYLE

SERVES 4

245 Kcals per portion

2 (200-g) cans mackerel steaks in brine, drained
2 dessert apples, diced
2 teaspoons lemon juice
4 spring onions, diced
4 celery sticks, sliced
freshly ground black pepper
300 ml/$\frac{1}{2}$ pint natural yogurt
cayenne

Mix the mackerel with the apples, lemon juice, spring onions, celery and black pepper to taste. Arrange the mixture on a serving dish. Cover with the yogurt and chill in a refrigerator for 1 hour.

Sprinkle with cayenne before serving with cream crackers.

SCANDINAVIAN FISH SALAD

SERVES 6 TO 8

110 Kcals per portion

1 (200-g) can shrimps, drained
1 (200-g) can prawns, drained
2 (105-g) cans smoked mussels, drained
225 g/8 oz button mushrooms, thinly sliced
225 g/8 oz tomatoes, cut in wedges
225 g/8 oz frozen petits pois, cooked and drained
1 small lettuce, shredded, to serve
Mustard Dressing
2 tablespoons mild prepared mustard (for example, Dijon)
4 tablespoons salad oil (try sunflower oil)
3 tablespoons lemon juice
salt and pepper
$\frac{1}{4}$ *teaspoon sugar*

Toss the fish with the mushrooms, tomatoes and petits pois. Combine all the ingredients for the dressing in a screw-topped jar and shake well. Pour over the salad and mix lightly. Serve on a bed of shredded lettuce.

COOK'S TIP

All fish canned in oil uses vegetable oil – an unsaturated oil that is particularly good as part of a healthy diet.

KIPPER SCRAMBLES

SERVES 2

430 Kcals per portion

If you have a microwave oven in your kitchen then you may be quite used to making scrambled eggs in it; if you are not familiar with microwaved scrambled eggs, then follow the micro-tip below.

3 eggs
3 tablespoons milk
salt and pepper
1 (198-g) can kipper fillets, drained
25 g/1 oz butter
2 slices freshly buttered toast
chopped parsley
grilled tomato halves

Beat together the eggs, milk and seasoning. Remove the skin from the kippers and then flake the fish. Melt the butter in a saucepan over a moderate heat, add the egg mixture and stir until lightly set. Stir in the kipper fillets, and turn immediately on to the hot toast. Garnish with parsley and serve with tomatoes.

◈ MICRO-TIP

To cook this recipe in the microwave, beat the eggs and milk in a basin with seasoning to taste. Add the butter and cook on high for 2–4 minutes. Whisk the eggs twice during cooking and remove them from the microwave when slightly undercooked. Stir in the kipper fillets and serve. Heat the tomato halves in the microwave for 30–60 seconds.

SARDINE OPEN SANDWICHES

SERVES 2

225 Kcals per portion

50 g/2 oz cucumber, finely chopped

$\frac{1}{2}$ teaspoon salt

2 slices pumpernickel

butter

lettuce leaves

1 (120-g) can sardines, drained

1 tablespoon finely chopped onion

2 tablespoons soured cream

Worcestershire sauce

lemon twists

paprika

Put the cucumber in a sieve and sprinkle the salt over it. Leave for 10 minutes. Spread the pumpernickel with butter and top with lettuce leaves. Split the sardines and arrange on the lettuce. Press the excess moisture from the cucumber through the sieve, then mix the cucumber with the onion, soured cream and a dash of Worcestershire sauce. Spoon this mixture on top of the sardines and garnish with a lemon twist and sprinkling of paprika.

Topping Ideas for Open Sandwiches

Open sandwiches are delicious as a quick snack, for a light lunch or for supper. Try some of the following ideas for tasty toppings.

Salmon and Cucumber: Start with a thin layer of shredded lettuce, add flaked red salmon and diced cucumber. Season and sprinkle with a little lemon juice.

Prawns and Cream Cheese: Spread the bread with cream cheese, top with prawns or shrimps and sprinkle with snipped chives.

Tuna Special: Top the bread with flaked tuna (or

use sandwich tuna if you prefer), then add onion rings, sliced tomato and black olives.

Devilled Crab: Season dressed crab with a little mustard and Worcestershire sauce. Spread on bread and top with cucumber.

Anchovy and Tomato: Top the bread with sliced tomato, anchovy fillets and olives.

Sardine Special: Cover the bread with cucumber slices. Flake drained sardines in oil with seasoning, then pile on top of the cucumber. Add grated lemon rind for colour and flavour.

Skipper Creams: Top the bread with skippers and garnish with tomato. Add a little soured cream and parsley sprigs.

Smoked Mackerel with Lemon: Top the bread with smoked mackerel fillets and sprinkle with lemon juice. Season with ground black pepper. Garnish with cucumber and lemon.

Smoked Oysters Supreme: Top the bread with smoked oysters, sliced hard-boiled eggs and sliced stuffed green olives. Sprinkle with lemon juice and parsley.

HOT TOASTIES

SERVES 2 TO 4

Toasted snacks are always popular and here you will find ideas for toasted sandwiches as well as toast toppers.

Sardine Specials
Mash 1 (120-g) can sardines in tomato sauce with 50 g/2 oz grated cheese. Spread over 2 slices Granary bread and top each with a second slice of Granary. Brown on both sides under the grill then serve at once.

Skipper Poachers
Drain 1 (106-g) can skippers in oil and arrange on 2 slices freshly toasted bread. Put under a moderate grill to heat through; meanwhile, poach an egg to serve on each. Serve with a green salad, if you like.

Spicy Pilchard Sandwiches
Mash 1 (215-g) can pilchards in tomato sauce with 1 teaspoon curry powder, adding seasoning to taste. Spread over 4 slices bread, top with sliced tomatoes and a second slice of bread. Brown both sides under a moderate grill, then serve freshly cooked.

Sild and Cucumber
Drain and mash 1 (110-g) can of sild in oil with 2 tablespoons finely chopped cucumber or gherkins. Sandwich between slices of bread then toast slowly on both sides.

Tuna and Horseradish
Mash 1 (100-g) can tuna in oil with 1 teaspoon horseradish sauce and a little parsley. Sandwich between wholemeal bread and toast on both sides.

Salmon Pockets
Warm 2 pieces pitta bread under the grill. Cut a slit in each and open out the pocket. Mash 1 (105-g) can pink salmon with 1 tablespoon fruit chutney and 1 teaspoon tomato purée. Divide between the pitta bread pockets and heat through under the grill before serving.

SNACK-PACK PITTA

SERVES 4

140 Kcals per portion

Flat, oval-shaped pitta breads are ideal for snacks – when cut down one side, the bread can be separated slightly to give pockets. If you like, heat the pitta bread first, putting it under a hot grill for a few minutes without allowing it to brown.

4 pitta breads
1 (120-g) can sardines in oil, drained and mashed
3 tablespoons diced cucumber
4 tomatoes, deseeded and quartered
4 white cabbage leaves, shredded
lemon juice
salt and pepper

Split open the pitta breads to make pockets. Mix the sardines with the cucumber, tomatoes and cabbage. Season with lemon juice, salt and pepper. Pack the mixture into the pitta breads.

Variation Replace the sardines with 1 (200-g) can smoked mackerel fillets. Alternatively use 1 (120-g) can sardines in tomato sauce or 1 (185-g) can sandwich tuna.

SKIPPER SPECIALS

SERVES 2

200 Kcals per portion

2 slices rye bread
1 tablespoon cream cheese
1 (106-g) can skippers in tomato sauce
1 small green dessert apple, cored and sliced

Spread the rye bread with the cream cheese. Arrange the skippers diagonally over the cream cheese, interspersed with the sliced apple.

Variation Use crispbread instead of rye bread and sprinkle with a little chopped dill.

TUNA AND FRUIT IN SOUR MUSTARD SAUCE

SERVES 4

250 Kcals per portion

Tuna and chopped fruit are combined in a tangy sauce to make an unusual, light snack. Have some crispbread or crackers, French bread or pitta bread as an accompaniment if you are feeling really hungry.

1 (200-g) can tuna steak in oil or brine, drained
2 dessert apples, cored and diced
1 orange, cut into segments
1 banana, sliced
shredded white cabbage leaves
Sauce
6 tablespoons soured cream
1 tablespoon milk
1 tablespoon lemon juice
1 teaspoon caster sugar
$\frac{1}{2}$ *teaspoon salt*
1 tablespoon prepared mustard
freshly ground black pepper

Blend the sauce ingredients together. Toss the tuna and fruit in the sauce. Serve on a bed of shredded white cabbage leaves.

SPECIAL SALMON ROLL

SERVES 4

258 Kcals per portion

Well-filled bread rolls really are a good snack – try some of the interesting wholemeal sesame-topped or grainy bread rolls that are now available. You can always vary the filling by using canned tuna instead and add a pinch of curry powder.

1 (213-g) can red salmon, drained and flaked
1 tablespoon mayonnaise
2 teaspoons sultanas
1 tablespoon finely diced onion
salt and pepper
4 large crisp rolls, split
shredded lettuce leaves

Combine the salmon with the mayonnaise, sultanas, onion, salt and pepper. Cover the bases of the rolls with shredded lettuce leaves and divide the salmon mixture on top. Replace the tops of the rolls.

HEALTH BUNS

SERVES 1

370 Kcals per portion

If you want a light snack, then make the filling and have just one bun. The rest of the filling can be stored, in a covered basin or carton, in the refrigerator until the next day.

2 Granary or wholemeal buns, split
25 g / 1 oz butter or low-fat spread
1 (185-g) can tuna chunks in brine, drained and flaked
2 tablespoons cottage cheese
1 celery stick, finely chopped
3 walnut halves, chopped
1 tablespoon mayonnaise
$\frac{1}{2}$ teaspoon grated horseradish

Spread the buns with the butter or low-fat spread. Mix the tuna with the remaining ingredients. Divide the mixture between the buns. Serve with a crisp celery stick.

COOK'S TIP

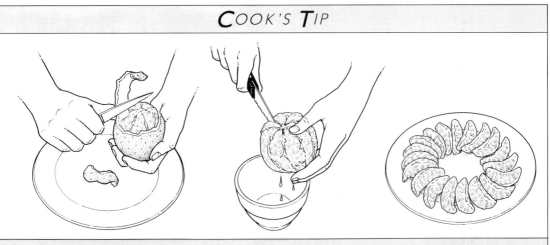

Orange segments taste best if they are cut away without any of the membranes or pips.
1 To do this, first cut off all the peel and pith.

2 Hold the orange over a basin to catch the juice, then use a small sharp serrated knife to cut between the

membranes that separate the segments. Cut in towards the middle of the fruit on both sides of each segment.

3 The orange segments are delicious as a topping for open sandwiches, with smoked canned fish, or for salads.

17

GOING SOLO

It is sometimes difficult to work up enough enthusiasm to create a meal for yourself. Remember that eating alone need not be a dreary occasion, so plan a meal you particularly enjoy and lay the table – or a tray – attractively.

All the recipes in this chapter have been written to suit the single person – some offer a substantial portion for when you have a hearty appetite, others are geared towards days when the calorie count is being carefully controlled! You will also find all the recipes easy to prepare.

When you are shopping for yourself look for the convenient smaller-sized cans of fish or plan in advance to turn a larger can into two tasty meals. Include some fresh vegetables on your shopping list and buy some rice and pasta too. Read through the recipe ideas in this chapter and you will surely feel inspired to treat yourself to a special meal.

SAVOURY STUFFED EGGS

SERVES 1

370 Kcals per portion

This interesting stuffing for hard-boiled eggs turns them into a tempting and satisfying meal. When in season, you may like to cook some new potatoes as an accompaniment, otherwise just have some bread and butter. Remember that you can always open a large can of fish and save half the contents for another recipe or just to serve on toast.

2 hard-boiled eggs
1 (155-g) can pilchards in brine, drained
50 g/2 oz cucumber, grated
2 tablespoons single cream
1 teaspoon sesame or celery seeds
salt and pepper
2 tomatoes, quartered
green salad (lettuce, watercress, green pepper)

Cut the eggs in half. Remove the yolks and mash them with the pilchards. Dry the cucumber on absorbent kitchen paper, then add with the cream, sesame or celery seeds and seasoning to the fish mixture. Pipe or spoon this into the egg whites. Serve with the tomatoes and green salad.

Variations Other canned fish can be used in this recipe. Use 1 (120-g) can sardines in oil, drained. Alternatively, use 1 (50-g) can anchovies, drained, and add 4 tablespoons mayonnaise instead of the cream.

Left: Tuna-stuffed Peppers (page 21) and Salmon-stuffed Tomatoes (page 20)

SALMON-STUFFED TOMATOES

SERVES 1

380 Kcals per portion
(Illustrated on page 18)

When they are in season try those large beefsteak tomatoes for this recipe — they have plenty of flavour and hold an ample portion of filling.

2 large tomatoes
1 (105-g) can pink salmon, drained and flaked
1 celery stick, chopped
1 small or $\frac{1}{2}$ medium onion, chopped
$\frac{1}{2}$ packet white sauce mix
150–250 ml/5–8 fl oz milk
1 teaspoon lemon juice
salt and pepper
1–2 tablespoons fine, fresh breadcrumbs

Cut a small lid from the rounded end of the tomatoes. Scoop out the seeds and pulp from the centre and discard.

Combine the salmon with the celery and onion. Make up the sauce according to the instructions on the packet, using the milk. Add to the salmon mixture with the lemon juice, salt and pepper, and mix well. Fill each tomato with as much of the fish mixture as possible — any remaining is ideal for serving on toast — and sprinke with breadcrumbs. Place under a moderate grill for 10–15 minutes until golden and bubbling.

◈ MICRO-TIP

The sauce can be cooked in a large basin in the microwave. Place the sauce mix in the basin, then whisk in the milk. Cook on high for 5–7 minutes, until boiling and thickened. Whisk twice during cooking. Continue as above. The tomatoes are best browned under the grill but they can be heated through in the microwave on high for 2–3 minutes. The cooking time depends on the size of the tomatoes.

SARDINE-STUFFED MUSHROOMS

SERVES 1

320 Kcals per portion

These are great for times when you really do not want to spend hours in the kitchen but feel the need for a hot meal. Make some crunchy toast to go with the stuffed mushrooms or just have a simple tomato salad as an accompaniment.

2 large flat mushrooms
1 (120-g) can sardines in oil
25 g/1 oz Cheddar cheese, grated

Wipe the mushrooms clean with damp absorbent kitchen paper. Brush the mushrooms with 2 teaspoons of the oil from the sardines. Flake the fish and pile on the cups of the mushrooms. Sprinkle with the cheese. Place under a low grill for 10 minutes. Increase the heat to high to brown the cheese just before serving.

COOK'S TIP

A simple tomato salad is often the best accompaniment for a variety of fish dishes. If you have the time peel the tomatoes (see page 27), otherwise just slice them and place on a plate or shallow dish. Allow 2 tomatoes per person. Sprinkle with seasoning, a tiny pinch of caster sugar, some chopped chives or finely chopped onion and a little chopped parsley if you like. Dress with a sprinkling of oil (try olive oil or sunflower oil) and a little wine vinegar. Leave for about 15 minutes for the flavours to mix well before serving.

TUNA-STUFFED PEPPER

SERVES I

297 Kcals per portion
(Illustrated on front cover and page 18)

This recipe is a good one to prepare in advance – make the stuffing, blanch the peppers and combine in an ovenproof dish. Cover and store in the refrigerator, then bake for 20 minutes.

25 g/ I oz brown rice
I large green pepper
25 g/ I oz sweetcorn
I (100-g) can tuna steak in oil, drained
2 tablespoons chicken stock
salt and pepper
lemon wedges to garnish

Put the rice in a saucepan and add water to cover the grains generously. Bring to the boil, then reduce the heat slightly and cover the pan. Cook for about 25–30 minutes, or until the grains are tender. Drain thoroughly and leave to cool.

Cut the pepper in half lengthways, remove the core and seeds, and blanch in boiling water for 3 minutes. Combine the rice, sweetcorn and tuna, moisten with the stock and add seasoning. Fill the pepper halves with the mixture. Put into an ovenproof dish, cover with a lid or cooking foil and cook in a moderately hot oven (190C, 375F, gas 5) for 20 minutes. Garnish with lemon before serving.

COOK'S TIP

Canned fish is available in a variety of sizes so look out for the one that suits you best. This way you avoid any waste.

PILCHARD BAKE

SERVES I

590 Kcals per portion

I large potato, freshly baked
25 g/ I oz butter
salt and pepper
I (155-g) can pilchards in brine, drained
25 g/ I oz Cheddar cheese, grated

Cut a lengthways slice from the top of the potato. Scoop out the floury middle of the potato into a basin and mash with the butter and seasoning. Pack this mixture into the potato shell. Cover with the pilchards and sprinkle the grated cheese on top. Place under a moderate grill until golden.

SILD WITH POTATO TOPPING

SERVES I

520 Kcals per portion

2 medium potatoes, cooked
I egg
I (110-g) can sild in tomato sauce
4 mushrooms, thinly sliced
3 tablespoons cider
40 g/ 1½ oz Cheddar cheese, grated

Mash the potatoes with the egg. Lay the sild on the base of an ovenproof dish, cover with the mushrooms and pour over the cider. Pipe or fork the mashed potato over the fish mixture. Sprinkle with the cheese. Heat under a moderate grill for 10 minutes, then increase the heat to brown the potato before serving.

◈ MICRO-TIP

Cook the potatoes in their jackets in the microwave oven, allowing about 7–8 minutes on full power. Assemble the dish as above and cook on full power for 2–3 minutes.

SAVOURY SARDINE SPECIAL

SERVES 1

---

450 Kcals per portion

A creamy coleslaw salad or juicy vegetable dish, like cauliflower or leeks in cheese sauce, would go very well with this sardine and rice dish. It offers a good way of using up any small amounts of leftover cooked rice, or why not substitute diced cooked potato if you have some?

---

1 tablespoon oil
1 small onion, chopped
1 celery stick, chopped
1 (120-g) can sardines in tomato sauce
50 g/2 oz cooked long-grain rice
2 tablespoons white breadcrumbs
15 g/½ oz Cheddar cheese, grated

Heat the oil in a frying pan. Add the onion and celery, and cook until soft but not browned. Stir in the sardines and rice and heat through.

Turn the mixture into a flameproof dish and sprinkle the breadcrumbs and cheese on top. Place under a hot grill for 2–3 minutes until the breadcrumbs are golden brown and the cheese has melted. Serve with vegetables or salad.

◈ MICRO-TIP

Mix the oil, onion and celery in a large basin. Cook, uncovered, on high in the microwave for 4–5 minutes. Stir in the sardines and rice and cover. Heat on high for 2–3 minutes. Top with the browned breadcrumbs and cheese and microwave for 30 seconds or use white breadcrumbs and brown under the grill as above.

TUNA AND BROCCOLI BAKE

SERVES I

460 Kcals per portion

100 g / 4 oz frozen broccoli, cooked
15 g / ½ oz butter
I (100-g) can tuna steaks in brine, drained
I tomato, quartered
salt and pepper
Cheese Sauce
15 g / ½ oz butter
I tablespoon flour
6 tablespoons milk
pinch of mustard powder
salt and pepper
50 g / 2 oz Cheddar cheese, grated

Arrange the cooked broccoli in the base of an ovenproof dish and dot with the butter. Place the tuna and tomato on top and season well.

Put the butter, flour, milk, mustard and seasoning in a saucepan. Bring to the boil, stirring all the time, and cook until the sauce has thickened. Add 40 g / 1½ oz of the cheese and pour over the tuna and tomato, leaving a border of broccoli showing round the edge. Sprinkle the remaining cheese on top and bake in a moderately hot oven (200 C, 400 F, gas 6) for about 25–30 minutes, or until golden brown. Serve hot.

◈ MICRO-TIP

Frozen broccoli cooks very well in the microwave oven. Arrange the frozen spears in a dish, placing the thick stems towards the edge of the dish and the florets in the middle. The outer edge of the dish receives more microwave energy than the middle so the tough stems will cook well. Cover the dish and cook on high for about 4–5 minutes, or until tender. Leave to stand for 2 minutes.

HERRINGS FLORENTINE

SERVES 1

450 K cals per portion

On its own this dish is full of flavour and low in calories – the perfect meal for when you are keeping an eye on your diet.

175 g / 6 oz frozen spinach
1 tablespoon soured cream
garlic salt and pepper
1 (200-g) can herring fillets in tomato sauce
25 g / 1 oz Cheddar cheese, grated
paprika

Cook the spinach as directed on the packet. Drain and mix with the soured cream and seasoning. Put the spinach mixture in a flameproof dish. Lay the herring fillets on top and sprinkle with the grated cheese and paprika. Place under a moderate grill until the cheese is melted and golden.

DEVILLED HERRING ROE

SERVES 1

210 K cals per portion

These tasty herring roes also taste good on thick slices of hot buttered toast.

25 g / 1 oz butter
1 small onion, chopped
½ teaspoon prepared English mustard
dash of Worcestershire sauce
1 (225-g) can tomatoes
garlic salt and pepper
1 (125-g) can soft herring roes

Melt the butter in a small saucepan. Add the onion and cook until soft but not browned. Stir in the mustard, Worcestershire sauce and tomatoes. Season with garlic salt and pepper, stir well, then add the drained herring roe. Heat through gently, then serve with cooked rice or pasta.

SAVOURY CRUMBLE

SERVES 1

620 K cals per portion

If you think of crumbles as beng restricted to sweet recipes, then try this tempting idea and you will be pleasantly surprised!

100 g / 4 oz cauliflower sprigs
2 celery sticks, cut into 2.5-cm / 1-in lengths
salt
1 (125-g) can mackerel fillet in tomato sauce
1 tablespoon milk
Topping
25 g / 1 oz margarine
50 g / 2 oz plain flour
25 g / 1 oz Cheddar cheese, grated

Put the cauliflower and celery in a saucepan, add salt, cover with boiling water and cook for 10–15 minutes, or until just tender. Drain well and put in an ovenproof dish with the mackerel steaks. Mix some of the tomato sauce from the fish with the milk and pour over the mackerel steaks.

To make the topping, rub the margarine into the flour until it resembles breadcrumbs and then add the cheese. Spread the topping over the fish mixture and cook in a moderately hot oven (200 C, 400 F, gas 6) for 15–20 minutes.

Variation Use the cheesy crumble topping given in the above recipe for a variety of bases.

For a salmon and spinach base, melt 15 g/½ oz butter or margarine in a saucepan, then stir in 1 tablespoon flour and 250 ml/8 fl oz milk. Bring to the boil stirring all the time. Drain and flake 1 (105-g) can pink salmon. Defrost and thoroughly drain 225 g/8 oz frozen spinach, then stir it into the sauce with the salmon. Season to taste and pour into an ovenproof dish. Top with the crumble and bake as in the main recipe.

COOK'S TIP	
Mackerel fillet in tomato sauce are a versatile ingredient – they can be turned into	a tasty curry (see page 65). Flaked and seasoned they are delicious on toast.

PRAWNS BASQUE STYLE

SERVES 1

400 Kcals per portion

Next time you feel like treating yourself to a special meal, try this recipe – it's very easy to cook and makes a substantial meal.

25 g / 1 oz butter
1 small onion, chopped
1 garlic clove, crushed
1 small green pepper, deseeded and chopped
1 tablespoon tomato purée
1 (227-g) can tomatoes
pinch of dried thyme
1 (100-g) can prawns, drained
salt and pepper
75 g / 3 oz hot cooked rice

Heat the butter in a saucepan. Add the onion, garlic and green pepper, and cook until soft but not browned. Stir in the tomato purée, tomatoes and thyme. Cover and simmer for 15 minutes, stirring occasionally. Add the prawns and seasoning, and cook for a further 3–5 minutes. Spoon the prawn mixture on to a bed of rice and serve immediately.

SKIPPER CELERY KEBABS

SERVES 1

360 Kcals per portion

4 celery sticks, cut into 3.5-cm / 1½-in lengths
salt and pepper
50 g / 2 oz mushrooms
1 (106-g) can skippers in oil, drained
2 small tomatoes, quartered
1 teaspoon grated onion
1–2 tablespoons lemon juice or vinegar
dash of chilli sauce
175 g / 6 oz hot cooked spinach

Cook the celery in boiling salted water for 20 minutes, or until just tender. Drain well. Halve any large mushrooms. Put the skippers in the celery pieces. Thread the filled celery pieces, mushrooms and tomatoes alternately on to metal skewers. Mix the onion, lemon juice or vinegar, seasoning and chilli sauce, spoon over the kebabs and leave to marinate for 30 minutes.

Place under a moderate grill and cook for 3–4 minutes on each side. Serve on a bed of cooked spinach.

COOK'S TIP

Ten easy ways to turn tuna into a meal
Drain 1 (100-g) can tuna and try these ideas.

1 Flake it into freshly cooked rice. Add some chopped spring onion and season with a little chilli. Good with natural yogurt!

2 Flake it into a portion of freshly cooked pasta. Stir in 2 tablespoons cream, natural yogurt or mayonnaise and season with black pepper.

3 Turn the fish out on to a flameproof dish. Top with 1 chopped tomato and some grated cheese – or a slice of mozzarella. Put under a moderate grill to heat through and brown. Great with cooked rice, pasta, potatoes or salad.

4 Add to 1 (227-g) can tomatoes and heat through. Season, then serve with cooked rice, pasta or canned red kidney beans.

5 Mix into mashed potato, adding a little grated cheese. Put into a flameproof dish and top with cheese. Grill until golden, serve at once.

6 Turn out on to a lettuce leaf. Top with mayonnaise and grated lemon rind.

7 Mix with diced cooked potato or cooked pasta and mayonnaise. Season with a little paprika.

8 Mix with chopped celery, chopped apple and cooked rice. Sprinkle with the oil from the can and a dash of lemon juice.

9 Flake into a dish and top with chopped green or black olives, chopped onion and sliced tomato. Sprinkle with oil and lemon juice.

10 Mix with 1 (227-g) can butter beans or red kidney beans and a little chopped onion. Dress with the oil from the can, seasoning and lemon juice.

FAMILY FAVOURITES

Here is a chapter full of practical recipes to please all the family. From fish cakes and croquettes to bakes, pies and cobblers—all are included. For times when you feel like preparing a special treat there are recipes for pancakes filled with tuna, a delicious savoury ring mould and a special salmon pie.

These recipes are all economical enough to make delicious everyday meals that are both nutritious and satisfying but will not tie you to the kitchen for hours on end. Many of the dishes include helpful serving suggestions and some need little in the way of accompaniments. So, next time you're short of inspiration for mid-week family dinners have a look through these ideas and you will come up with some winners, soon to be family favourites, no doubt!

CELERY AND TUNA SOUP

SERVES 4

110 Kcals per portion

A wholesome, warming soup makes an excellent family meal. The combination of tuna and celery gives this recipe a good flavour.

350 g/ 12 oz celery, roughly chopped
4 tomatoes, peeled, deseeded and diced
50 g/ 2 oz onion, diced
1 garlic clove, crushed (optional)
450 ml/$\frac{3}{4}$ pint boiling water
600 ml/ 1 pint skimmed milk
1 blade of mace
1 bay leaf
1 (185-g) can tuna chunks in brine, drained
4 teaspoons cornflour
salt and pepper
Garnish
chopped tomato
chopped parsley

Put all the ingredients, except the cornflour and seasoning, into a large saucepan. Bring to the boil and simmer for 15 minutes. Remove the blade of mace and bay leaf. Blend the soup in a liquidiser until smooth.

Mix the cornflour with a little of the soup to make a smooth cream. Return the soup to the rinsed-out saucepan, add the cornflour mixture and stir over a low heat until the soup thickens. Check the seasoning and garnish before serving.

COOK'S TIP

To peel tomatoes, place them in a basin and cover with freshly boiling water. Leave for 30–60 seconds, then drain and peel. The peel should slip off very easily once it is pierced with a knife.

If you want to peel just one or two tomatoes, then skewer them on to the end of a fork and hold over a gas flame until lightly charred. Rinse under the cold tap and rub off the peel.

Left: Mustard Pilchard Layer (page 29)

SALMON CAKES

SERVES 4

160 Kcals per portion

1 (213-g) can pink salmon, drained and flaked
225 g/8 oz potatoes, cooked and mashed
2 tablespoons natural yogurt
finely grated rind of 1 lemon
1 tablespoon chopped parsley
2 tablespoons finely chopped celery
wholemeal flour for coating
2 tablespoons vegetable oil for frying

Combine the salmon, potatoes, yogurt, lemon rind, parsley and celery, and mix well. Divide the mixture into eight equal portions and form into flat cakes. Turn each fish cake in flour until it is evenly coated. Heat the oil in a frying pan and cook the fish cakes over a moderate heat until golden brown, turning once.

Variations
Tuna Cakes: Replace the salmon with 1 (185-g) can sandwich tuna.
Smoked Mackerel Cakes: Use 1 (200-g) can smoked mackerel fillets instead of the salmon. Instead of the yogurt you may like to try using 1 tablespoon creamed horseradish.
Tomato Pilchard Cakes: Omit the salmon and the yogurt. Mash 1 (215-g) can pilchards in tomato sauce with the sauce and use instead of the salmon.
Cod Roe Cakes: Use 2 (100-g) can soft cod roe (drained) instead of the salmon.

CAPTAIN'S CROQUETTES

SERVES 4

200 Kcals per portion

The secret of making good, light croquettes is to chill the fish mixture before shaping and coating it. If you ever have the time, then make a large batch of these and open freeze them when coated – they can be deep fried from frozen when you need them.

2 (110-g) cans sild in tomato sauce
15 g/½ oz margarine
25 g/1 oz flour
1 teaspoon lemon juice
salt and pepper
oil for deep frying
1 egg, beaten
50 g/2 oz breadcrumbs

Drain the tomato sauce from the sild and reserve. Mash the fish with a fork. Heat the margarine in a saucepan over a low heat, stir in the flour and cook for 1 minute. Add the reserved tomato sauce and lemon juice, and cook for 2 minutes, or until the sauce becomes thick. Mix in the mashed fish and add seasoning. Leave to cool, then chill well.

Heat the oil to 180 C/350 F in a deep frying pan. Divide the fish mixture into eight equal portions and shape into croquettes. Dip each croquette in the beaten egg and then in the breadcrumbs. Fry in the hot oil until golden brown and drain on absorbent kitchen paper.

Serve with parsley sauce or tartare sauce.

COOK'S TIP

Step-by-step to Perfect Croquettes

1. Turn the cooked mixture into a dish and cool. Chill well.
2. Take a portion of the mixture and shape it on a well-floured surface. Use two palette knives or one knife and a fish slice to pat the mixture into shape.
3. Coat in egg and breadcrumbs, then pat back into shape. The croquettes are ready for cooking. Leave them in the refrigerator if you are not ready to cook them.

MACKEREL FILLETS AU GRATIN

SERVES 4

200 Kcals per portion

This unusual recipe is tasty and satisfying – cut the bread quite thickly for hungry members of the family. You can make your own sauce (try following the Cook's Tip below) or use a packet mix. Sweetcorn or peas, or a mixture of both, make a good accompaniment.

oil for frying
I small onion, finely chopped
2 (125-g) cans mackerel fillets in brine,
drained
4–6 slices bread
450 ml/$\frac{3}{4}$ pint white sauce, heated
100 g/4 oz Cheddar cheese, grated
paprika

Heat a little oil in a frying pan. Add the onion and cook until soft but not browned. Mash the mackerel fillets and the onion together in a basin. Set aside.

Toast the bread and spread each slice with the fish mixture. Spoon the white sauce evenly over the mackerel and sprinkle with the cheese. Sprinkle lightly with paprika and place under a moderate grill until bubbling hot and lightly browned.

MUSTARD PILCHARD LAYER

SERVES 4

210 Kcals per portion
(Illustrated on page 26)

This tasty bake takes only a few minutes to prepare – you can always assemble it in the baking dish, then cover and keep it in the refrigerator until you are ready to bake it. Baked or mashed potatoes are good accompaniments.

I (425-g) can pilchards in brine, drained
I tablespoon mustard powder
300 ml/$\frac{1}{2}$ pint natural yogurt
4 courgettes, thinly sliced
4 tomatoes, thinly sliced
2 medium onions, diced
50 g/2 oz Cheddar cheese, grated
chopped parsley

Fork the pilchards roughly with the mustard and blend in the yogurt. Put half the pilchard mixture in an ovenproof dish, arrange the courgettes, tomatoes and onions on top and cover with the remaining fish mixture. Sprinkle with the cheese. Bake in a moderate oven (180C, 350F, gas 4) for 30 minutes, or until golden. Sprinkle liberally with parsley before serving.

Variations You may like to try using herring fillets in savoury sauce instead of the pilchards in the above recipe. Alternatively, mackerel fillets in brine give an equally delicious result.

COOK'S TIP

If you often have problems with lumpy sauces, then try this one-stage method: sprinkle 25 g/I oz flour into a saucepan and very slowly whisk in 450 ml/$\frac{3}{4}$ pint milk. Whisk hard to avoid lumps. Add a knob of butter and seasoning, then cook over a moderate heat, whisking continuously. As the milk begins to steam, reduce the heat slightly and continue whisking until the sauce boils. Cook for 2–3 minutes, then flavour as required or serve.

◇ MICRO-TIP

This bake can be made in the microwave oven. Cook the onions with I tablespoon oil in a basin first, allowing 5 minutes on full power. Assemble the dish as above then cook on full power for 12–15 minutes. Brown the top under the grill.

PILCHARD PIE

SERVES 4 TO 6

395 Kcals per portion

To make your own pastry follow the instructions given in the Cook's Tip (right).

225 g / 8 oz shortcrust pastry
1 tablespoon oil
1 large onion, chopped
100 g / 4 oz mushrooms, sliced
1 (425-g) can pilchards in brine, drained
2 tablespoons chopped parsley
4 tablespoons tomato chutney
1 egg, beaten

Roll out two-thirds of the pastry and use to line a 20-cm/8-in flan ring or pie plate.

Heat the oil in a frying pan. Add the onion and mushrooms and cook until soft but not browned. Mash the pilchards with the parsley and spread half over the pastry case. Cover with the onion mixture and then top with the chutney and remaining pilchard mixture. Roll out the remaining pastry and cut into long strips. Arrange these in a lattice pattern on top of the pie. Brush with the beaten egg and bake in a moderately hot oven (200 C, 400 F, gas 6) for 20–25 minutes until golden.

Serve hot or cold with vegetables or salad.

Variations You may like to try some of the following tasty combinations.
Sardine and Sweetcorn: Add drained canned sardines in oil and use sweetcorn relish.
Mackerel and Apple Chutney: Use drained mackerel in brine instead of the pilchards and add apple chutney instead of the tomato chutney.

CORNISH PIE

SERVES 4

500 K cals per portion

Richly-flavoured pilchards marry well with tangy apple and onion in this unusual savoury plate pie. Serve creamy mashed potatoes or buttered new potatoes as an accompaniment.

225 g/8 oz shortcrust pastry
I cooking apple, peeled and sliced
I onion, thinly sliced
I (425-g) can mackerel in tomato sauce, drained
salt and pepper
milk

Halve the pastry and roll out each piece to fit a 20-cm/8-in pie plate. Line the plate with one piece. Put half the apple and onion on the base. Arrange the pilchards on top. Cover with the remaining apple and onion, adding seasoning.

Moisten the edge of the pastry with water, place the pastry lid on the pie and pinch together the edges to seal in the filling. Brush with milk and bake in a moderately hot oven (200 C, 400 F, gas 6) for 20–25 minutes. Serve piping hot.

COOK'S TIP

Perfect Shortcrust Pastry

1 Put 225 g/8 oz plain flour in a bowl. Add 100 g/4 oz margarine. Using fingertips, rub the fat into the flour until the mixture resembles fine breadcrumbs.

2 Use a round-bladed knife to mix in about 3–4 tablespoons water, a spoonful at a time. Use just enough water to bind the dry mixture.

3 When the mixture begins to clump together use your fingertips to gather it into a ball. Press together lightly, wrap in cling film or a polythene bag and chill for 10 minutes before using. This quantity is referred to as **225 g/8 oz shortcrust pastry**.

SPICY HERRINGS

S E R V E S   4

200 Kcals per portion

Cook up a taste of the Orient with this interesting recipe. If you would like to extend the flavour through the meal, then why not stir-fry some bean sprouts with onions and shredded cabbage?

1 tablespoon cooking oil
1 medium onion, sliced into rings
generous pinch of ground ginger
pinch of garlic salt
1 tablespoon soy sauce
1 teaspoon sugar
juice of $\frac{1}{2}$ lemon
2 (200-g) cans herring fillets in savoury sauce
4 tablespoons water

Heat the oil in a frying pan. Add the onion and cook until soft but not browned. Add the ginger and garlic salt and cook for 1 minute. Stir in the soy sauce, sugar and lemon juice. Add the herring fillets, rinse out the can with the water and pour over the fish. Heat through for 5–10 minutes, then serve on a bed of boiled rice.

HARVEST PILCHARDS

S E R V E S   4

250 Kcals per portion

Quick-fried, finely shredded white cabbage mixed with a little chopped onion makes a good accompaniment for this wholesome pilchard dish.

175 g/ 6 oz potatoes, thinly sliced
1 (425-g) can pilchards in brine, drained
225 g/ 8 oz cooking apples, peeled and thinly sliced
2 teaspoons grated lemon rind
275 ml/ 9 fl oz cider
4 tomatoes, thinly sliced

Par-boil the potatoes (for about 10 minutes) and drain. Put the pilchards and apples in a saucepan over a low heat and cook for 10 minutes, stirring frequently. Then put the fish mixture in an ovenproof dish and cover with the sliced potatoes.

Sprinkle the grated lemon rind on top and pour over the cider. Arrange the tomatoes decoratively on top. Bake in a moderate oven (180 C, 350 F, gas 4) for 45 minutes, or until the potatoes are tender.

SAVOURY SARDINE PIE

S E R V E S   4

280 Kcals per portion

2 (120-g) cans sardines in brine, drained and flaked
4 hard-boiled eggs, chopped
600 ml/ 1 pint white sauce
1 (397-g) can tomatoes, drained
salt and pepper
1 kg/ 2 lb potatoes, boiled and mashed
50 g/ 2 oz butter
1 egg, beaten

Mix the sardines with the eggs and white sauce. Add the tomatoes and stir in seasoning to taste. Put into an ovenproof dish.

Beat the potatoes with the butter and egg. Add seasoning. Spread or pipe the potatoes over the fish mixture. Bake in a moderately hot oven (190 C, 375 F, gas 5) for 20–30 minutes until golden. Serve with peas, cut French beans or sweetcorn.

Variations Try some of these tasty alternatives. *Smoked Fish Pie:* Use smoked mackerel fillets in oil instead of the sardines in the above recipe. *Tuna and Mushroom Pie:* Use tuna chunks in oil or brine instead of the sardines and stir in 100 g/4 oz sliced mushrooms instead of the tomatoes.

TUNA AND POTATO BAKE

SERVES 4

275 Kcals per portion

1 kg/2 lb potatoes
salt and pepper
225 g/8 oz onions, thinly sliced
1 (185-g) can tuna chunks in oil, drained
300 ml/½ pint milk
50 g/2 oz Cheddar cheese, grated

Cut the potatoes into large even-sized pieces and put them in a saucepan of cold, salted water. Bring to the boil and simmer for 10 minutes. Drain immediately and slice the potatoes thickly.

Layer the potatoes, onions and tuna in a greased ovenproof dish, seasoning between each layer and finishing with a layer of potatoes. Pour the milk over, then sprinkle with the grated cheese. Place in a moderately hot oven (200 C, 400 F, gas 6) for 45 minutes, or until the vegetables are tender when tested with a skewer.

Variation If you like smoked fish, then you will find that smoked mackerel fillets taste very good cooked in the above recipe instead of the tuna. You will need 1 (200-g) can.

◈ *MICRO-TIP*

This recipe can be cooked in the microwave oven – cook the potatoes with 2 tablespoons water in a covered dish for about 10–15 minutes on full power. Cook the onions with the oil from the tuna, on full power for 5–7 minutes. Assemble the ingredients as above, using 150 ml/ ¼ pint milk and cover the dish. Cook on full power for 7–10 minutes, then sprinkle with the cheese and brown under the grill.

SAVOURY RING MOULD

SERVES 4

330 Kcals per portion

This is another one of those recipes that is easy to make, good to eat and a little bit different. Surround the mould with cooked peas if you like and serve with boiled or creamed potatoes.

4 (110-g) cans sild in tomato sauce
50 g/2 oz butter
50 g/2 oz plain flour
150 ml/¼ pint milk
2 eggs
salt and pepper
1 (397-g) can tomatoes, chopped with their juice

Drain and reserve the tomato sauce from the sild. Mash the fish. Melt the butter in a saucepan. Stir in the flour, then gradually pour in the milk stirring continuously. Keep the saucepan over a low heat and bring to the boil, stirring continuously until the mixture becomes very thick. Remove from the heat, cool slightly, then beat in the eggs, one at a time, and season. Fold in the sild.

Pour the mixture into a 20-cm/8-in buttered ring mould and cover with buttered paper or kitchen foil. Place in a moderate oven (170 C, 325 F, gas 3) for 45 minutes or until the mixture is firm.

Heat the reserved tomato sauce with the chopped tomatoes, adding seasoning to taste. Unmould the ring on to a warm plate and top with the hot tomato sauce.

◈ *MICRO-TIP*

This recipe can be cooked in the microwave oven. First prepare the sauce by whisking the butter, flour and milk together in a basin. Cook on full power for 2–4 minutes. Continue as above, using a microwaveproof ring mould. Cover with absorbent kitchen paper and microwave on full power for 5–7 minutes. Leave to stand for 5 minutes before turning out.

MACKEREL LOAF

SERVES 4

---

180 Kcals per portion

---

2 (125-g) cans mackerel fillets in brine,
drained and mashed

---

50 g/2 oz fresh wholemeal breadcrumbs

---

1 egg, beaten

---

2 tablespoons natural yogurt

---

25 g/1 oz gherkins, chopped

---

2 teaspoons lemon juice

---

1 tablespoon chopped parsley

---

salt and pepper

Garnish

---

lemon slices

---

cucumber slices

Combine all the ingredients and mix well. Put into a greased 450-g/1-lb loaf tin and smooth the top. Stand the loaf tin in a roasting tin and pour in sufficient boiling water to come half-way up the sides of the outer tin.

Bake in a moderate oven (180 C, 350 F, gas 4) for 45 minutes, or until the loaf is browned on top and slightly shrunk away from the sides of the tin. Allow the loaf to cool in the tin before turning out.

Serve garnished with lemon and cucumber.

Variations

Tuna and Mushroom Loaf: Use 1 (200-g) can of tuna in brine instead of the mackerel. Add 100 g/4 oz finely chopped mushrooms and omit the yogurt. Bake as above.

Sardine and Spinach Loaf: Substitute 2 (120-g) cans of sardines in oil for the mackerel. Defrost and thoroughly drain 225 g/8 oz frozen chopped spinach. Mix all the ingredients and bake as above.

◈ *MICRO-TIP*

This loaf cooks well in the microwave. Instead of the metal tin use a 450-g/1-lb loaf dish. Microwave on high, uncovered, for about 7 minutes, or until the loaf has shrunk away from the sides of the dish and feels firm in the middle.

CHEESY SALMON BAKE

SERVES 4

250 Kcals per portion

This is a favourite family dish that adapts well to special occasions. Simply divide the ingredients between four individual ovenproof dishes and serve with soured cream and chopped chives.

225 g/8 oz frozen spinach, thawed
salt and pepper
pinch of grated nutmeg
3 tomatoes, sliced
1 (440-g) can pink salmon, drained and flaked
50 g/2 oz wholemeal breadcrumbs
50 g/2 oz Cheddar cheese, grated
25 g/1 oz butter or margarine
Garnish (optional)
lemon slices · tomato slices

Season the spinach with salt, pepper and nutmeg. Put into a 1-litre/1¾-pint ovenproof dish. Arrange the tomatoes on top and cover with the salmon. Mix the breadcrumbs and cheese together and sprinkle over the fish. Dot with the butter or margarine and bake in a moderately hot oven (200 C, 400 F, gas 6) for 25 minutes, or until crisp and golden on top.

COOK'S TIP

Keta salmon is also an economical alternative to red salmon. It is lower in calories and ideal for a variety of family dishes where a colourful appearance is not as vital as a winning flavour.

SARDINE COBBLER

SERVES 4

385 Kcals per portion

Cobblers are wholesome dishes to satisfy raging appetites. This is a very easy recipe and the scone topping is given extra texture by the addition of a few oats. Serve with green vegetables but there is no need to add potatoes or pasta.

2 (120-g) cans sardines in tomato sauce
2 tablespoons water
Scone Topping
50 g/2 oz margarine
250 g/9 oz self-raising flour
1 tablespoon rolled oats
250 ml/8 fl oz milk

Put the sardines with the water into a shallow ovenproof dish.

Rub the fat into the flour, add the rolled oats and bind to a pliable dough with the milk. Roll out the dough to 1-cm/$\frac{1}{2}$-in thickness. Use a 5-cm/2-in diameter pastry cutter to stamp out circles and arrange these overlapping on top of the sardines. Place in a moderately hot oven (200 C, 400 F, gas 6) for 20–25 minutes until golden.

Variations Other varieties of canned fish can be used to make delicious cobblers. For example, try herrings in savoury sauce or pilchards in tomato sauce. If you like, add some quick-fried vegetables to the fish before adding the cobbler topping – thinly sliced leeks, sliced mushrooms and chopped celery can be added, or try one of the many types of frozen mixed vegetables that are available.

TUNA LASAGNE

SERVES 4

350 Kcals per portion

1 (397-g) can tomatoes, drained
1 tablespoon tomato purée
1 teaspoon dried marjoram
salt and pepper
1 (400-g) can tuna chunks in brine, drained
175 g/6 oz lasagne strips
25 g/1 oz butter
4 teaspoons cornflour
300 ml/$\frac{1}{2}$ pint milk
50 g/2 oz Cheddar cheese, grated
2 teaspoons grated Parmesan cheese

Put the tomatoes, tomato purée, marjoram, salt and pepper into a saucepan and simmer for 30 minutes. Add the tuna.

Meanwhile cook the lasagne in boiling salted water for 10–15 minutes. Drain.

Melt the butter in a saucepan over a low heat, add the cornflour and cook for 1 minute. Then blend in the milk and bring to the boil. Add seasoning. Remove from the heat and stir in the Cheddar cheese.

Arrange half the cooked lasagne on the base of an ovenproof dish. Top with the tomato and tuna mixture. Cover with the remaining lasagne. Pour the cheese sauce over the lasagne and sprinkle with the Parmesan cheese. Place in a moderately hot oven (200 C, 400 F, gas 6) for 30–35 minutes until golden and bubbling.

COOK'S TIP

Canned sild, skippers, herrings, kippers, sardines, pilchards, mackerel are all rich sources of proteins, vitamins and minerals which are essential for good health.

HOT TUNA PANCAKES

SERVES 4

300 K cals per portion

Pancakes
100 g / 4 oz plain flour
pinch of salt
1 egg
250 ml / 8 fl oz milk
oil for frying
Filling
1 (185-g) can tuna chunks in brine, drained
2 spring onions, finely diced
3 tablespoons natural yogurt
1 teaspoon horseradish cream
Topping
5 tablespoons natural yogurt
75 g / 3 oz Cheddar cheese, grated
dash of Worcestershire sauce

Sift the flour with the salt into a bowl. Make a well in the middle, add the egg and beat in the milk gradually, working in the flour to form a smooth batter. Beat well, then leave to stand for a while – if you have the time, leave the batter for 30 minutes.

To cook the pancakes, heat a little oil in a non-stick frying pan. Pour in just enough batter to cover the base of the pan. Cook until set and lightly golden on the underside. Flip the pancake over and cook on the other side. Using a lightly greased pan each time, make eight pancakes.

Mix the ingredients for the filling together. Spread over the prepared pancakes and roll each one up like a Swiss roll. Place in a flameproof dish.

Mix the ingredients for the topping together and pour over the pancakes. Place under a moderate grill for 10 minutes, or until heated and golden.

Variations Other types of canned fish that make mouthwatering fillings for pancakes include salmon (try keta salmon, for example), sild and smoked mackerel. For special pancakes add smoked oysters or mussels and prawns or shrimps.

COOK'S TIP

Soft cod roe makes a good savoury sauce to serve with hard-boiled eggs. To make a hot dish, make 300 ml / ½ pint savoury white sauce (see page 29), then stir in 2 tablespoons chopped parsley and 1 (100-g) can cod roe. Beat well. Pour over the hard-boiled eggs and serve with rice, mashed potatoes or pasta.

COOK'S TIP

Pancakes freeze well and they are almost as easy to make in large quantities as they are a few at a time. So when you have the time, make up two or three times the quantity of batter (remember to use a liquidiser if you have one) and cook the pancakes.

Layer the pancakes, placing pieces of kitchen paper or special freezer leaves between each one. You can remove as many pancakes as you need by sliding a palette knife between them when frozen.

STUFFED COURGETTES

SERVES 4

120 Kcals per portion

4 large courgettes
1 (185-g) can tuna chunks in oil
1 onion, finely diced
4 tomatoes, peeled and diced
2 teaspoons chopped parsley
$\frac{1}{2}$ teaspoon dried thyme
salt and pepper
25 g/ 1 oz breadcrumbs
25 g/ 1 oz Cheddar cheese, grated (optional)

Par-boil the courgettes for 10 minutes. Drain and cut in half lengthways. Scoop out the pulp and cut into dice. Put the hollowed-out courgettes in an ovenproof dish.

Drain the tuna and reserve the oil. Fry the onion in the reserved tuna oil until soft. Add the tomatoes, parsley, thyme, salt and pepper. Fill this mixture into the hollowed-out courgettes and sprinkle with the breadcrumbs. Cover with cooking foil and place in a moderate oven (350 F, 180 C, gas 4) for 15 minutes.

For an extra crunchy topping, sprinkle with the cheese in addition to the breadcrumbs and remove the cooking foil after 10 minutes in the oven.

Variations: This stuffing can also be used for aubergines, cabbage leaves, peppers or tomatoes. *Aubergines* – halve 2 aubergines, scoop out the middle and chop, then sprinkle with salt and leave for 30 minutes. Rinse and dry on absorbent kitchen paper, then fry with the onion. Continue as above. *Cabbage Leaves* – blanch 4 large cabbage leaves in boiling stock for 3–5 minutes, then drain. Divide the fish mixture between the leaves and fold each into a neat package. Continue as above. *Peppers* – halve and scoop out the seeds from 2 peppers. Blanch in boiling water for 2–3 minutes, then place in an ovenproof dish and continue as above. *Tomatoes* – cut a slice off the tops of 4 large tomatoes and scoop out the seeds. Fill with the mixture and put under a medium hot grill until browned on top.

SPECIAL SALMON PIE

SERVES 4 TO 6

460 K cals per portion

375 g / 13 oz shortcrust pastry
1 (213-g) can red salmon
100 g / 4 oz frozen peas
4 tablespoons mayonnaise
freshly ground black pepper
beaten egg

Roll out two-thirds of the pastry to 5-mm/$\frac{1}{4}$-in thickness and use to line a 20-cm/8-in pie plate.

Mash the salmon in its oil, and add the peas, mayonnaise and black pepper. Spread the fish mixture over the pastry base.

Roll out the remaining pastry and cut into long strips. Arrange these in a lattice pattern on top of the pie. Brush with beaten egg. Place in a moderately hot oven (200 C, 400 F, gas 6) for 20—25 minutes until golden. Serve hot or cold.

SALMON PASTA

SERVES 4

490 K cals per portion

175 g / 6 oz pasta shapes
50 g / 2 oz butter or margarine
1 medium onion, sliced
1 red pepper, deseeded and chopped
1 (440-g) can red salmon, drained and flaked
1 (326-g) can sweetcorn, drained
1 tablespoon lemon juice
2 tablespoons chopped parsley
25 g / 1 oz flaked almonds, roasted

Cook the pasta shapes in plenty of boiling salted water for about 15 minutes, or until tender. Drain.

Meanwhile, melt the butter or margarine in a frying pan. Add the onion and red pepper, and cook until soft but not browned. Add the salmon to the pan with the sweetcorn and heat through, then add the pasta, lemon juice and parsley. Heat for a few minutes — the pasta does not take long to heat through — stirring gently. Serve at once sprinkled with the flaked almonds.

BAKED POTATOES

Stuffed baked potatoes are firm family favourites and they are so easy to make for a tasty supper. Scrub the potatoes and cut out any bad bits. Bake in a moderately hot oven (190C, 375F, gas 5) for about 1 hour, or until the potatoes are cooked through. (Test them with a fork). Try some of the filling ideas here; scoop out the soft middle and mash it with the ingredients suggested, then press the mixture back into the shells and brown under the grill.

Tasty Tuna
Mash the potato with sandwich tuna, a knob of butter and a little tomato purée. Add a little milk and seasoning. Top with grated cheese before grilling.

Skippers 'n' Tomato
Mash the potato with skippers in tomato sauce. Season and add a knob of butter.

Creamy Kippers
Mash the potato with a little white sauce, seasoning and butter. Mix in flaked kippers, parsley and a little Gruyère cheese. Top with extra grated cheese before grilling.

Sardine and Cheese
Mash the potato with drained sardines in oil and grated cheese, adding seasoning and milk to soften the mixture. Grill until golden.

◆ MICRO-TIP

Baked potatoes cook particularly quickly in the microwave oven – great for an express snack. Prick the skins to prevent the potatoes bursting during cooking. Put the potatoes as far apart as possible on the turntable or in the base of the oven on a double-thick piece of absorbent kitchen paper. Cook for the times given below.

Large Potatoes
(350 g/12 oz each)
1 potato   – 8 minutes
2 potatoes – 15 minutes
4 potatoes – 25–27 minutes

Medium-small potatoes
(175 g/6 oz each)
1 potato   – 4–6 minutes
2 potatoes – 6–8 minutes
4 potatoes – 10–12 minutes
6 potatoes – 18–20 minutes

PIZZA BASE

SERVES 4

225 g/8 oz self-raising flour
1 teaspoon baking powder
1 teaspoon mustard powder
$\frac{1}{2}$ teaspoon salt
pinch of cayenne
50 g/2 oz margarine
100 g/4 oz Cheddar cheese, finely grated
about 7 tablespoons milk
oil for frying

Put the flour, baking powder, mustard, salt and cayenne into a basin. Rub the margarine in until the mixture resembles breadcrumbs. Mix in the cheese and add sufficient milk to make a soft dough. Roll out on a floured board to a circle 1-cm/$\frac{1}{2}$-in thick. Fry in a large frying pan in a little oil until golden brown, turning once. Keep hot off the heat.

Tasty Toppings
Traditional Tomato: Fry 1 chopped onion in a little olive oil with 1 crushed clove garlic. Stir in chopped canned tomatoes and a little dried marjoram. Season and spread over the base. (Use this as a base for many other ingredients.) Top with a lattice of anchovy fillets, black olives and the oil from the anchovies. Grill to heat through.
Tuna and Cheese: Make the tomato topping as above, spread over the base and add flaked tuna. Sprinkle with grated cheese or chopped mozzarella and grill until golden.
Sardine and Spring Onion: Spread the base with tomato topping (as above), then arrange sardines on top and sprinkle with chopped spring onions. Add grated cheese and grill until golden.
Salmon and Mushroom: Top the base with sliced fresh tomatoes, flaked pink salmon and sliced mushrooms. Sprinkle with grated cheese and grill.
Pilchard and Oregano: Top the base with flaked pilchards, a little oregano, sliced tomatoes and cheese. Grill to brown.
Seafood Spectacular: (illustrated on front cover) Top with the traditional tomato topping. Arrange anchovy fillets like the spokes of a wheel on top. Add flaked tuna, smoked mussels and oysters, baby clams, prawns and mozzarella cheese. Top with an olive and grill to brown.

TUNA SWEET AND SOUR SALAD

SERVES 4

250 Kcals per portion

2 (200-g) cans tuna in oil
2 onions, finely chopped
2 tablespoons tomato purée
250 ml/8 fl oz cider
7 tablespoons water
I tablespoon demerara sugar
2 tablespoons Worcestershire sauce
2 tablespoons chutney
salt and pepper
2 teaspoons arrowroot
To Serve (optional)
I small lettuce, washed and shredded, or
225 g/8 oz long-grain rice, cooked and cooled

Heat the oil from the tuna in a frying pan. Add the onions and cook until soft but not browned. Add the tomato purée, cider, water, sugar, Worcestershire sauce, chutney, salt and pepper. Bring to the boil and simmer, uncovered, for 20 minutes. Mix the arrowroot with a little liquid from the pan and stir in to thicken the sauce. Season and cool.

Toss the tuna in the cold sauce. To serve, divide the mixture between four individual plates arranging it on shredded lettuce or cold cooked rice tossed with a well-seasoned Vinaigrette dressing.

PILCHARD SALAD

SERVES 4

385 Kcals per portion

For a light meal or supper dish serve the salad with bread rolls or French bread. If you want a more substantial meal then serve with baked potatoes. The juice from the pineapple makes a refreshing drink when chilled.

150 g/5 oz white cabbage, finely shredded
I (340-g) can pineapple cubes in natural juice, drained
I small onion, thinly sliced
2 dessert apples, cored and thinly sliced
150 ml/¼ pint mayonnaise
I (425-g) can pilchards in tomato sauce
Garnish
6 black olives, stoned
25 g/1 oz walnuts, chopped
chopped parsley

Mix the cabbage, pineapple, onion and apples with the mayonnaise. Arrange on a serving dish and put the pilchards and tomato sauce in the centre. Garnish with the olives, walnuts and chopped parsley.

Variations Smoked mackerel fillets or herrings in tomato sauce are also tasty in this salad. Sprinkle the smoked mackerel with a little lemon juice before serving.

COOK'S TIP

Salad Dressings with a Difference

A tempting, speedy meal can be prepared by simply opening a can of sardines in oil, smoked mackerel fillets, pilchards in brine, tuna steak or pink or red salmon and arranging the fish on a plate with a few slices of tomato, cucumber or lettuce leaves. Add a touch of home cooking with one of these interesting dressings if you like and serve with bread and butter. Remember that the oil from the can gives the dressing a good flavour.

Vinaigrette – place 6 tablespoons oil and 2 tablespoons wine vinegar in a screw-topped jar. Add 2 teaspoons prepared mustard (try whole-grain, Dijon or a slightly smaller amount of English), ½ teaspoon sugar, plenty of salt and pepper and, if you like, some chopped parsley. Shake well to combine the ingredients. This dressing can be stored in the refrigerator for several days, or for up to a month without the fresh parsley.

Mayonnaise Ideas – make bought mayonnaise taste a bit different by adding chopped fresh herbs (parsley, lemon balm, mint, thyme or chives), a crushed garlic clove, some finely chopped salted peanuts or walnuts; finely crumbled blue cheese or finely grated cucumber also go very well.

FUN FISH FOR KIDS

Canned fish is ideal for the younger members of the family who usually prefer the delicate taste of traditional favourites like tuna and salmon. The recipes in this chapter are created to persuade the most difficult of eaters to try a variety of fish.

Canned fish is full of the goodness that growing families need – protein, vitamins and minerals are preserved in the can. Calcium – an essential mineral for the healthy development of bones and teeth – is rich in those canned fish where the edible bones are eaten, for example in salmon and sardines.

Remember too that John West canned fish is additive free so it is an ideal food for introducing into the toddler's diet. In this chapter recipe servings are calculated for kids' appetites.

SURFBOARDERS

SERVES 4 TO 6

200 Kcals per portion

450 g/ 1 lb potatoes, cooked and mashed
1 egg, beaten
50 g/ 2 oz self-raising flour
1 (106-g) can skippers in oil, drained and mashed
plain flour
beaten egg or milk to glaze
butter to serve

Mix the potatoes with the egg, flour and mashed skippers. Roll out the mixture on a floured board to 1-cm/½-in thickness. Use a 5-cm/2-in diameter pastry cutter to stamp out circles. Place the circles on a baking tray, brush with a little beaten egg or milk and cook in a moderately hot oven (100 C, 400 F, gas 6) for 10–15 minutes until golden.

Use ovengloves to remove the tray from the oven, then transfer the cakes to a wire rack. Cool slightly, then eat while still hot, spread with butter.

TIPS FOR YOUNG COOKS

Cut out a variety of different shapes from the mixture. To do this use some of the shaped cutters that are available or cut out a small cardboard template to use as a guide.

Left: Sardine Beananza (page 44)

FISH HATS

SERVES 4

230 Kcals per portion

---

4 bread rolls

50 g/2 oz butter, softened

1 (110-g) can sild in tomato sauce

1 dessert apple, cored and chopped

Cut a thin slice from the top of the rolls and reserve. Scoop out the soft centre to leave a crisp shell.

Mash the butter and sild together with the sauce from the can. Mix in the apple and pack into the roll shells. Replace the tops, and wrap each filled roll in a square of cooking foil. Place on a baking sheet in a moderately hot oven (200C, 400F, gas 6) for 15 minutes.

TIPS FOR YOUNG COOKS

You will find it is easy to use your fingers to pull out the soft middle of the rolls. Make sure you wash your hands first and take care not to pull away too much bread or you may break the outer crust. The middle bit can be dried and saved in an airtight jar or made into breadcrumbs and frozen – ask mum what she wants to do with it.

SARDINE BEANANZA

SERVES 4

250 Kcals per portion
(Illustrated on page 42)

---

1 (440-g) can baked beans

2 (120-g) cans sardines in tomato sauce

450 g/1 lb potatoes, sliced and par-boiled

25 g/1 oz butter, melted

Put the baked beans into an ovenproof dish. Cover with the sardines. Arrange the sliced potatoes overlapping on top. Brush with the melted butter. Bake in a moderately hot oven (200C, 400F, gas 6) for 30 minutes, or until golden.

Remember to use ovengloves to remove the hot dish from the oven.

TIPS FOR YOUNG COOKS

Par-boiled potatoes are cooked in boiling salted water for about 10 minutes, or until they are half cooked. Remember to do this first, before making the rest of the recipe.

FLYING SAUCERS

SERVES 4

250 Kcals per portion

Straight from the oven, these flying saucers are red hot – so take care when eating them. Served up with spaghetti Invaders they make a great meal for youngsters and they are full of the protein and minerals that growing children need.

2 burger buns, halved
1 (185-g) can sandwich tuna
2 tomatoes, halved
4 slices cheese

Spread each bun half with sandwich tuna and place on a greased baking tray. Top each with a tomato half, rounded side uppermost. Place a piece of cheese on top of each – the cheese will not fit neatly at this stage but it will coat the tomato as it melts.

Cook the flying saucers in a moderately hot oven (200 C, 400 F, gas 6) for 15 minutes, until lightly browned and bubbling. Use a fish slice to transfer the hot flying saucers to plates and serve.

COOK'S TIP

The bones in sardines, skippers, sild and salmon are all edible – avoid removing them because they provide essential calcium. Mash or flake the fish with the soft bones and you will not even notice them.

TUNA BURGERS

SERVES 4

190 Kcals per portion

These tasty tuna burgers are an excellent alternative to beefburgers and they can be served in the same way. This recipe provides plenty of protein, vitamins and minerals.

1 (185-g) can tuna chunks in oil
4 large potatoes, cooked and mashed
2 onions, finely chopped
100 g/4 oz celery, finely chopped
1 tablespoon finely chopped capers (optional)
1 tablespoon chopped parsley
1 teaspoon Worcestershire sauce
salt and pepper
1 teaspoon grated lemon rind
seasoned flour for coating
oil for brushing

Mash the tuna in its oil and add to the potatoes with all the remaining ingredients, seasoning well. Shape the mixture into eight round burgers. Dust with flour. Brush lightly with oil and place under a moderate grill for about 6 minutes on each side.

Tasty Burger Toppings
You can add lots of different burger toppings if you like.
Toasted Cheese: Top with a slice of cheese before grilling the second side.
Tomato and Onion: Add slices to the cooked burgers, serve in buns.
Cream Cheese and Relish: Spread a bun with cream cheese and top the burger with relish.

KIPPER DIPPERS

SERVES 4

130 Kcals per portion

1 (200-g) can kipper fillets, drained

1 tablespoon horseradish sauce

2 teaspoons lemon juice

1 tablespoon chopped parsley

pepper

7 tablespoons natural yogurt

To Serve

carrot sticks

celery sticks

apple slices

crisps

Mash the kippers with a fork and combine with the horseradish sauce, lemon juice, parsley, pepper to taste and yogurt. Put in a small bowl and chill in the refrigerator. Serve on a large plate surrounded by the raw vegetables, apple and crisps.

SALMON SUBMARINES

SERVES 2

245 Kcals per portion

Take care when eating toasted cheese because it really is very hot!

4 bridge rolls, cut in half

1 (105-g) can pink salmon, drained

1 tablespoon natural yogurt

4 slices processed cheese

2 tomatoes, sliced

Toast the cut surfaces of the bridge rolls. Mash the salmon with the yogurt. Spread the mixture over the rolls. Cover with a slice of cheese and top with sliced tomatoes. Place under a moderate grill until golden brown.

HEDGEHOGS IN TOMATO SAUCE

S E R V E S   4

230 Kcals per portion

1 (185-g) can tuna chunks in oil, drained and flaked
1 egg, beaten
100 g/4 oz parsley and thyme stuffing mix
50 g/2 oz long-grain rice
1 (295-g) can condensed tomato soup, diluted
chopped parsley

Mix the tuna with the egg, stuffing mix and rice. Shape into small balls in the palm of your hand – the mixture will make about 16.

Put the soup into a saucepan. Add the tuna balls and simmer, covered, for 20–25 minutes, until the rice is cooked. Check during cooking and add extra water if necessary. Serve sprinkled with parsley.

TUNA NESTS

S E R V E S   4

310 Kcals per portion

1 kg/2 lb potatoes, cooked and mashed
50 g/2 oz cheese, grated
1 (440-g) can baked beans
1 (185-g) can tuna chunks in brine, drained
4 spring onions, chopped
cucumber slices to garnish

Beat the potato and cheese together thoroughly, then spoon the mixture into a piping bag fitted with a large star nozzle. Pipe four oval-shaped potato nests on to plates and put under a moderate grill to heat and brown.

Heat the beans with the tuna and spring onions. Divide the tuna and bean mixture between the nests and serve at once. Add cucumber slices to garnish as shown.

SARDINE ROLLERS

SERVES 4

220 K cals per portion

These can also be made with pink salmon or tuna.

2 tablespoons mayonnaise
6 thin slices bread, crust removed
1 (120-g) can sardines in tomato sauce, mashed
melted butter

Spread the mayonnaise over the bread. Spread the sardines over the mayonnaise. Roll up each slice of bread like a Swiss roll and secure with two wooden cocktail sticks. Put on a baking tray. Brush with melted butter. Cut the rolls in half with a sharp knife. Place in a moderately hot oven (200 C, 400 F, gas 6) for 10 minutes.

FISH SIZZLERS

SERVES 4

120 K cals per portion

1 (120-g) can sardines in oil, drained and mashed
50 g / 2 oz Cheddar cheese, grated
1 (227-g) can tomatoes, drained
4 slices toast

Mix the sardines with the cheese and tomatoes. Spread the mixture over the toast and place under a moderate grill until sizzling. Cut into fingers and eat immediately, taking care not to burn your tongue!

COOK'S TIP

Shaping Sardine Rollers

1 Spread the filling over the bread and roll up firmly.

2 Secure the rolls with wooden cocktails sticks.

3 Cut each roll in half. Take a sharp knife and use a sawing action to avoid squeezing the filling out of the rollers.

WILD WEST SUPPER

SERVES 4

150 Kcals per portion

1 (440-g) can spaghetti in tomato sauce
1 (225-g) can pilchards in tomato sauce, flaked
1 small packet crisps, crushed
50 g / 2 oz Cheddar cheese, grated

Mix the spaghetti with the pilchards and put into an ovenproof dish. Mix the crisps with the cheese and sprinkle over the top. Place in a moderate oven (180 C, 350 F, gas 4) for 15 minutes, or until golden brown.

Variations

You can make this scrumptious supper dish using a variety of other canned fish. Try pink salmon, skippers, tuna, sardines or sild. Instead of the spaghetti you can also use baked beans. Alternatively, why not try some of the unusual canned spaghetti shapes that are available.

---

*T*IPS FOR *Y*OUNG *C*OOKS

You can crush the crisps in the packet before it is opened. Do this gently with your fingers taking care not to burst the bag or the crisps will fly out everywhere!

SKIPPER CAKES

SERVES 6

260 Kcals per portion

225 g / 8 oz self-raising flour
pinch of salt
25 g / 1 oz margarine
75 g / 3 oz Cheddar cheese, grated
2 (106-g) cans skippers in oil
6 tablespoons milk
1 tablespoon tomato ketchup
1 teaspoon Worcestershire sauce

Sift the flour and salt into a basin. Rub the fat into the sifted flour and add 25 g / 1 oz of the cheese.

Drain the skippers and reserve the oil. Flake the fish and add to the flour mixture with the milk, tomato ketchup and Worcestershire sauce. Mix to a dough. Roll out to an 18-cm/7-in circle and cut into eight wedges.

Arrange the wedges in a circle on a greased and floured baking tray, overlapping the edges. Brush with the reserved skipper oil and sprinkle with the remaining cheese. Place in a moderately hot oven (200 C, 400 F, gas 6) for 50 minutes, or until well risen and browned.

Serve hot with extra tomato sauce or pickles.

---

*T*IPS FOR *Y*OUNG *C*OOKS

Whenever you are baking something, just before you take the food out of the oven clear a space on the work surface ready to put the hot tin or dish down. Remember to put a table mat on the surface first. And use oven gloves.

PACK UP A TREAT

One of the real treats of summer is being able to eat outside, and the fresh air is guaranteed to perk up the appetite. Picnic food does not have to be limited to sandwiches made hours in advance and the recipes in this chapter provide practical, tempting ideas.

Quite apart from the special treat of summer, there are all those daily packed lunches. Flans, pasties and salads can be turned into packed lunches for variety instead of sandwiches and rolls.

Throughout the chapter there are tips on how to keep food fresh and how to pack food that is likely to become crushed in the picnic basket. Remember that the easiest of picnic fare comes straight from the can – take a can of salmon, tuna or skippers to eat with French bread, tomatoes and celery.

HERRING AND RICE SALAD

SERVES 2

300 Kcals per portion

100 g/4 oz long-grain rice, cooked and cooled
2 tomatoes, coarsely chopped
$\frac{1}{2}$ green pepper, deseeded and sliced
1 celery stick, finely sliced
1 (200-g) can herring fillets in savoury sauce
salt and pepper

Mix the rice, tomatoes, green pepper and celery with the savoury sauce from the herrings. Add seasoning.

Put the rice mixture in a plastic container and lay the herrings on top.

TUNA SALAD

SERVES 4

140 Kcals per portion

1 lettuce
1 (200-g) can tuna steak in oil, drained
1 red pepper, deseeded and thinly sliced
1 green pepper, deseeded and thinly sliced
1 (227-g) can pineapple rings in natural juice, drained and chopped
cocktail onions
vinaigrette dressing (optional)

Wash the lettuce and use the leaves to line a plastic container. Separate the tuna into fairly large chunks and combine with the peppers, pineapple and a few cocktail onions. Pile the mixture on to the lettuce and put the lid on the container.

If you are going to take some dressing, then keep it separate in a tightly-lidded container to add to the salad at the last minute.

Left: Tuna Triangles (page 56) and Sardine Pâté

SAILOR'S SALAD

SERVES 4

170 Kcals per portion

Canned beans make good, satisfying salads and they improve with standing so are perfect for picnics. You could always try canned red kidney beans or chick peas in this salad.

2 (120-g) cans sardines in vegetable oil
1 tablespoon cider vinegar
1 teaspoon paprika
1 (213-g) can butter beans, drained
1 large onion, thinly sliced
chopped parsley

Drain the sardines and reserve 2 tablespoons of the oil. Mix the oil with the vinegar and paprika. Toss the sardines very gently with the beans, onion and parsley in the dressing. Pack in an airtight container and stir lightly just before serving.

PICNIC TIP

Salads are good for both picnics and packed lunches but remember not to use any ingredients that are likely to discolour on standing. Avoid apples and avocados, for example, but take them with you to add at the last minute if you like.

Avocados are good picnic food – take them whole. Mash 1 (100-g) can tuna or 1 (110-g) can smoked mackerel fillets with some mayonnaise and a dash of lemon juice to make a tasty filling for the avocados. Pack this mixture in a small container or jar – remember to take a knife to cut the avocados in half and spoons to eat them.

SARDINE PÂTÉ

SERVES 4

225 Kcals per portion
(Illustrated on page 50)

1 (120-g) can sardines in oil, drained
150 g / 5 oz cream cheese
grated rind and juice of 1 lemon
1 teaspoon made mustard
pinch of paprika
freshly ground black pepper
1 tablespoon chopped fresh mixed herbs
(parsley, rosemary, thyme)
Garnish
lemon slices
fresh herbs

Mix all the ingredients together and beat until smooth.

Spoon the pâté into a container and smooth the top. Chill thoroughly and take on the picnic in a chiller bag, or tucked into a well-shaded corner of the picnic basket. Garnish before packing. Serve the pâté with crusty French bread.

PICNIC TIPS

Smooth, creamy fish pâtés are great for special picnics – they are easy to eat when spread on to French bread or with some biscuits. It is important to pack them well to make sure they stand up to the journey.

Put the pâté into a sturdy container, preferably a plastic one with a tight-fitting lid, and chill it really well beforehand so that the mixture firms up. If the container does not have a lid, then wrap it tightly in cooking foil or in a large piece of cling film to enclose the whole dish.

If you have a chiller bag, then put the pâté in it, otherwise wrap a folded, clean tea-towel round the outside of the container and put it in the picnic basket. The tea-towel will help to keep the pâté cool.

TUNA LOAF

SERVES 4

230 Kcals per portion

50 g / 2 oz margarine

I onion, finely chopped

I celery stick, finely chopped

50 g / 2 oz plain flour

375 ml / 13 fl oz milk

2 tablespoons mayonnaise

I teaspoon curry powder

squeeze of lemon juice

salt and pepper

2 tablespoons chopped parsley

I (185-g) can tuna chunks in brine, drained
and flaked

3 eggs

Heat the margarine in a heavy-based saucepan. Add the onion and celery and cook until soft but not browned. Add the flour and cook for I minute. Blend in the milk gradually and stir until the mixture boils and thickens. Remove from the heat. Add the mayonnaise, curry powder, lemon juice, salt and pepper, parsley and tuna. Allow the mixture to cool slightly, then beat in the eggs.

Put the mixture into a greased 450-g / I-lb loaf tin. Place in a moderate oven (180 C, 350 F, gas 4) for about I hour, or until the loaf shrinks slightly from the sides of the tin. Leave for I hour before turning out. Cut into slices and serve with a salad.

WHOLEMEAL PILCHARD FLAN

SERVES 4

245 Kcals per portion

75 g / 3 oz plain flour

pinch of salt

75 g / 3 oz wholemeal flour

40 g / 1½ oz lard · 40 g / 1½ oz butter

water to mix

Filling

100 g / 4 oz cottage cheese

2 eggs, beaten

salt and pepper

4 tablespoons milk

½ teaspoon mixed herbs

I (425-g) can pilchards in brine, drained

4 spring onions, chopped

Sift the plain flour and salt, add the wholemeal flour and rub in the fats until the mixture resembles breadcrumbs. Add sufficient water to mix to a firm dough. Roll out to 5-mm / ¼-in thickness and use to line a 20-cm / 8-in flan dish.

For the filling, mix the cottage cheese, eggs, seasoning, milk and herbs. Halve the pilchards, arrange in the pastry case and sprinkle the spring onions on top. Pour over the cottage cheese mixture. Place in a moderately hot oven (200 C, 400 F, gas 6) for 25–30 minutes until set and golden.

COOK'S TIP

Lining a Flan Dish

1 Use the rolling pin to lift the pastry over the dish.

2 Press the pastry neatly into the base and sides of the dish.

3 Roll the pin over the top of the dish to remove excess pastry round the edge.

Good sandwiches, with fresh bread and plenty of filling, make a satisfying and nourishing light meal. The key to making interesting sandwiches is to use your imagination – a cheese sandwich packed into a lunch box daily is hardly likely to tempt anyone!

Start with the bread: why not try different types of bread for a change? There are so many loaves available in most bakers or supermarkets that it is a shame not to make the most of them. If you think you are going to have problems cutting the bread thinly, then have a chunky sandwich instead – but make sure that there is plenty of filling in the middle.

Wholemeal or Granary breads are commonly used but rye bread or some of the richer breads also make good sandwiches. Use pitta bread, slit down one side to create a pocket for the filling, or pieces of French bread, slit lengthways. Remember those soft rolls, crisp breakfast rolls, finger rolls or Granary rolls. For extra large rolls try using sesame burger buns and for a very different result try slitting light croissants down one side.

Complete the sandwich pack by adding sticks of celery or carrot, an apple or a pear. Wrap the finished sandwich in cling film or put it in a closely fitting container to keep it in shape.

Now go on to the filling – some of these ideas should inspire you to create a sandwich feast!

Suggestions for Sandwich Fillings

1. Drain a can of salmon and mash the fish with grated cucumber and a little wine vinegar to taste.
2. Mix tuna with natural yogurt and season with horseradish sauce.
3. Mash sardines with a little mayonnaise and season to taste with curry powder.
4. Top flaked tuna with banana and tomato slices.
5. Cover shredded lettuce with salmon and avocado slices.
6. Chop hard-boiled eggs with sardines and chopped parsley.
7. Blend grated apple and flaked tuna or salmon with a little mayonnaise or natural yogurt.
8. Drain a can of salmon and mix with a light mustard sauce.
9. Mix tuna or sardines with chopped watercress and chutney.
10. Mix prawns and natural yogurt, season with tomato sauce and top with mustard and cress.

TRAWLER'S ROLL

SERVES 2

150 Kcals per portion

A sandwich with a difference – the grated apple mixed with the tangy yogurt and sardines is delicious and any browning of the apple will not be apparent.

4 slices wholemeal bread
1 (120-g) can sardines in brine, drained
1 tablespoon natural yogurt
½ green dessert apple, grated
2 gherkins, finely chopped

Remove the crusts from the bread. Mash the sardines with the yogurt, apple and gherkins. Spread this mixture over the bread and roll the bread (like a Swiss roll) over the filling. Secure with a cocktail stick. Pack into a plastic container.

FISH BITES

SERVES 4

230 Kcals per portion

1 (110-g) can sild in tomato sauce
2 large potatoes, cooked and mashed
1 egg
1 tablespoon chopped parsley
50 g/2 oz peanuts, finely chopped
50 g/2 oz fine wholemeal breadcrumbs
2 tablespoons lemon juice

Mash the sild and the sauce from the can with the potato, then beat in the egg and parsley. Form the mixture into 20 small balls. Mix the peanuts with the breadcrumbs on a plate. Roll each fish ball in the lemon juice, then in the peanut mixture. Arrange on a baking tray and bake in a moderately hot oven (200 C, 400 F, gas 6) for 10 minutes. Cool.

Pack the bites in a container lined with kitchen paper and take a small jar of mayonnaise as a dip.

Tuna Triangles

SERVES 4

355 Kcals per portion
(Illustrated on page 50)

175 g / 6 oz plain flour
pinch of mustard powder
salt and pepper
75 g / 3 oz margarine
75 g / 3 oz Cheddar cheese, grated
water
1 egg, lightly beaten
Filling
1 tablespoon oil
1 medium onion, finely chopped
1 (185-g) can tuna chunks, drained and flaked
2 teaspoons vinegar
salt and pepper
1 (455-g) can pineapple cubes in natural juice, drained
2 teaspoons plain flour
4 tablespoons single cream

Sift the flour, mustard powder, salt and pepper into a bowl, and rub in the fat until the mixture resembles fine breadcrumbs. Mix in the cheese and bind to a soft dough with water.

Prepare the filling. Heat the oil in a frying pan. Add the onion and cook until golden brown. Mix the tuna with the vinegar and pepper. Chop the pineapple cubes into small pieces. Combine the tuna, pineapple and onion, add the flour and put into a saucepan. Leave over a low heat for a few minutes, stirring occasionally. Remove from the heat, blend in the cream and season to taste.

Roll out the pastry on a floured board to 5-mm/ ¼-in thickness. Cut into 10-cm/4-in squares. Put a small amount of filling in the centre of each pastry square and fold over to form a triangle. Secure the edges and place on a damp baking tray. Brush the tops of the triangles with lightly beaten egg. Place in a moderately hot oven (200 C, 400 F, gas 6) for 20–25 minutes.

Finnish Fish Pasties

SERVES 6

360 Kcals per portion

These wholesome pasties are good for lunch boxes. With an apple or a stick or two of celery they provide a tempting mid-day snack.

375 g / 13 oz shortcrust pastry
1 egg, beaten
Filling
100 g / 4 oz cooked long-grain rice
1 tablespoon chopped parsley
1 tablespoon lemon juice
1 (185-g) can tuna chunks in oil, drained
salt and black pepper

Mix together the ingredients for the filling.

Roll out the pastry thinly on a floured board. Lay an inverted saucer on the pastry and run the tip of a sharp knife around it to cut a circle. Make 12 circles in this way. Put a generous tablespoon of the filling in a line along the centre of each circle. Moisten the edge of each circle with a little beaten egg, fold over like a Cornish pasty and pinch the edges together firmly. Brush with the remaining beaten egg. Place in a hot oven (220 C, 425 F, gas 7) for 10 minutes.

Variations You can also use skippers, smoked mackerel or kippers instead of the tuna in the filling for these pasties.

PICNIC TIP

Several types of fish come in ring pull cans that are perfect for taking on a picnic or for a tasty lunch at the office – good with a couple of tomatoes and some celery and easier than making sandwiches.

CORNISH SALMON AND CHEESE PASTIES

SERVES 6

400 Kcals per portion

450 g / 1 lb puff pastry

1 (440-g) can pink salmon, drained

4 medium shallots, finely chopped

1 teaspoon chopped parsley

100 g / 4 oz Caerphilly cheese, diced

3 tablespoons thick white sauce

salt and pepper

Roll out the pastry thinly on a floured board and leave it to 'rest' while preparing the filling.

Chop the salmon coarsely and mix with the remaining ingredients, seasoning lightly.

Lay an inverted 15-cm/6-in diameter plate on the pastry and run the tip of a sharp knife around it to cut a circle. Make six circles in this way. Place a sixth of the filling on one half of each pastry circle and moisten the edge of the pastry with cold water. Fold the uncovered pastry over the filling and press the top and bottom edges of the pastry together to seal them.

Place the pasties on a baking tray. Place in a hot oven (230 C, 450 F, gas 8) for 10 minutes, then reduce the heat to moderate (180 C, 350 F, gas 4) for a further 25 minutes. Cover the pasties loosely with cooking foil if they seem likely to become too brown as they cook. Transfer to a wire rack to cool.

COOK'S TIP

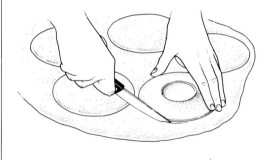

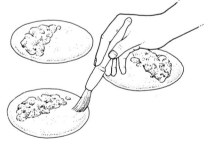

Making Pasties

1 Lay a small plate or saucer on the pastry and use a small pointed knife to cut out the circles. (For triangles cut out pastry squares.)

2 Cut out all the circles, then carefully lift away the excess pastry between the circles.

3 Divide the filling between the pastry circles, piling it neatly on one half of each. Dampen the edges with cold water.

4 Fold the uncovered pastry half over and press the edges together well to seal in the filling.

A TASTE OF THE WORLD

Variety is the spice of life and a little spice can certainly add variety to everyday cooking! Sample flavours from all over the world in this exotic chapter – sauces from Italy, rice from Spain or spices from India.

Canned fish can be used to create all sorts of delicious, authentic recipes from different corners of the world and you will find that many of these dishes are particularly versatile – some can be served as satisfying family meals or as good supper-party food. They also provide an ideal way of experimenting with the flavours of other cuisines since they are not particularly extravagant.

When you feel inclined to cook an exotic meal take a look at the ideas offered here and they will surely inspire you to create a foreign feast!

CALIFORNIAN FISH CHOWDER

SERVES 4 TO 6

190 K cals per portion

25 g / 1 oz butter
2 rashers rindless bacon, chopped
1 small onion, finely chopped
500 ml / 17 fl oz water or fish stock
2 teaspoons lemon juice
1 large potato, grated
salt and pepper
1 (185-g) can tuna chunks in brine, drained
25 g / 1 oz flour
250 ml / 8 fl oz milk
6 tablespoons single cream
Garnish
parsley or fennel
canned sweetcorn

Heat the butter in a heavy-based saucepan. Add the bacon and onion and cook until the onion is soft but not browned. Add the water or stock and lemon juice and bring to the boil. Add the potato, seasoning and tuna and simmer for 10 minutes, or until the potato is cooked. Blend the flour with the milk. Remove the soup from the heat, stir in the flour and milk mixture, then return to the heat and cook, stirring continuously, until thickened. Add the cream but do not allow the soup to boil again.

Serve garnished with parsley or fennel and sweetcorn.

Variation Use 1 (213-g) can pink salmon instead of the tuna chunks. Add (1 (400-g) can baby clams to make tasty clam chowder.

◆ MICRO-TIP

Soups cook well in the microwave oven. The secret of success is to add only a small quantity of liquid at the beginning of the cooking time, pouring in the rest when all the ingredients are cooked.

Left: Paella (page 64)

TONNATO SAUCE

SERVES 6 TO 8

640 Kcals per portion

Traditionally this sauce is served over cold sliced veal, garnished with capers, gherkins and lemon. It is also good with cold cooked chicken or used as a coating for halved hard-boiled eggs instead of plain mayonnaise.

4 egg yolks
500 ml/17 fl oz olive oil
1 (185-g) can tuna chunks in oil, drained
½ (50-g) can anchovy fillets, drained
pepper

Put the egg yolks into a basin. Add the oil gradually, whipping continuously until the mixture is thick and creamy.

Pound the tuna with the anchovy fillets and beat into the sauce. Add pepper to taste.

TARAMASALATA

SERVES 6

410 Kcals per portion

1 (200-g) can pressed cod roes
100 g/4 oz fresh white breadcrumbs, sprinkled with a little water
1 teaspoon salt
250 ml/8 fl oz oil
1 teaspoon tomato purée
juice of 1 lemon
1 large garlic clove, crushed
1 tablespoon grated onion
black olives

Thoroughly mash the cod roes with the moistened breadcrumbs and salt. Add the oil gradually, beating all the time to make a smooth creamy mixture. Stir in the tomato purée and lemon juice. Mix in the garlic and onion. Turn the mixture into a bowl and garnish with black olives.

Serve with pitta bread.

STUFFED TOMATOES À LA GRECQUE

SERVES 4

155 Kcals per portion

Throughout the countries of the Mediterranean, stuffed tomatoes are a popular dish. There are various fillings for the huge ripe tomatoes that grow in abundance; here is a tasty mixture of rice and sardines. Sandwich tuna, mackerel fillets or prawns can be used instead of the sardines if you like. Halve the quantities of rice and tomatoes if you want to serve them as a starter.

2 tablespoons olive oil
1 onion, chopped
1 large garlic clove, crushed
75 g/3 oz long-grain rice
300 ml/½ pint water
salt and pepper
1 (120-g) can sardines in oil
50 g/2 oz frozen peas
1 teaspoon marjoram
8 beefsteak tomatoes
bay leaf (optional)

Heat the oil in a saucepan. Add the onion and garlic and cook until soft but not browned. Add the rice and pour in 250 ml/8 fl oz of the water. Sprinkle in seasoning and bring to the boil. Cover the pan and reduce the heat, then simmer for 15–20 minutes or until most of the liquid has been absorbed, leaving the rice moist.

Flake the sardines and add them to the rice with the oil from the can. Add the peas and marjoram, then taste and adjust the seasoning.

Cut a slice off the tops of the tomatoes. Discard the stalk, chop the slices and add to the rice. Scoop the middle out of the tomatoes and chop it up, then add to the rice mixture. Place the tomatoes in an ovenproof dish and use a teaspoon to fill them with the rice mixture. Pour the remaining water into the dish and add the bay leaf (if used). Cover tightly with cooking foil and bake in a moderately hot oven (200 C, 400 F, gas 6) for 30 minutes. Serve at once.

MACKEREL DOLMADES STYLE

SERVES 4

90 Kcals per portion

Tasty, stuffed vine leaves are a standard feature on a Greek menu. Often filled with rice, there are many variations that include meat or fish. The cooked vine leaves can be served hot or cold, in which case they should be chilled before serving. A small dish of thick, Greek-style yogurt makes a good accompaniment.

2 (125-g) cans mackerel fillets in brine,
drained
2 tablespoons chopped red pepper
I tablespoon tomato purée
I teaspoon grated lemon rind
salt and pepper
8 large vine leaves
300 ml/½ pint fish stock
I tablespoon cornflour

Mash the mackerel fillets with a fork and mix with the red pepper, tomato purée, lemon rind and seasoning.

Put the vine leaves into a saucepan, cover with boiling water and cook gently for 2 minutes, or until the leaves are pliable. Drain and rinse the leaves in cold water. Remove any stalks. Put the leaves on a tea-towel to absorb the surplus moisture.

Divide the fish mixture between the vine leaves and fold up to enclose the filling. Put the stuffed vine leaves into a saucepan, packing them in neatly, and pour over the stock. Cover and cook very gently for 45–50 minutes. If the leaves are still slightly tough, cook for a few more minutes, adding a little water if necessary. Transfer the stuffed vine leaves to a serving dish and keep hot or allow to cool. Blend the cornflour with a little cold water, then add to the cooking liquid and bring to the boil, stirring continuously. Pour the sauce over the stuffed vine leaves and serve hot or allow to cool, then chill lightly before serving.

MEDITERRANEAN NOODLES

SERVES 4

350 Kcals per portion

Tomatoes, tuna and garlic are ingredients that are frequently used in Italian cooking – to top up a light pizza, to make a lively salad or, as in this recipe, to create a colourful pasta dish. Look out for fresh pasta, available in many supermarkets and most delicatessens, to serve instead of dried varieties. Remember to follow the packet instructions for the fresh pasta because it only needs brief cooking – about 3–5 minutes in boiling water.

I (397-g) can tomatoes
2 celery sticks, finely chopped
250 g/ 9 oz button mushrooms, wiped and sliced
I (200-g) can tuna in brine, drained and
broken into large pieces
I garlic clove, crushed
½ teaspoon mixed herbs or dried basil
salt and pepper
225–350 g/ 8–12 oz ribbon noodles

Put the tomatoes and celery in a saucepan and bring to the boil. Reduce the heat, cover and simmer for 5 minutes. Add the mushrooms, tuna, garlic, herbs, salt and pepper. Simmer for a further 10 minutes.

Meanwhile, cook the noodles in plenty of boiling salted water for about 15 minutes, or until tender but still firm. Drain and serve with the tuna sauce.

COOK'S TIP

Vine leaves are available in packets or cans from delicatessens and some good supermarkets. Although vine leaves are the traditional ingredient to use, you can also try wrapping this mackerel filling in blanched cabbage leaves. If you do use the cabbage leaves, then serve the cooked dish hot. Plain cooked rice and a simple tomato salad complete the meal very well.

COULIBIAC

SERVES 8

455 Kcals per portion

Coulibiac is a Russian fish pie, filled with hard-boiled eggs and rice (or sometimes other grains). Although it sounds exotic, it really does make an excellent family meal – it is full of goodness, and simple, familiar flavours are combined within the puff pastry crust. It tastes just as good cold as it does hot and in its native land would be served with some extra melted butter or soured cream. If you are conscious of dietary fibre, then you can always use brown rice and wholemeal puff pastry which is available frozen.

375 g/13 oz frozen puff pastry
1 (440-g) can red salmon, drained and flaked
50 g/2 oz butter, melted
3 hard-boiled eggs, chopped
1 tablespoon chopped parsley
salt and pepper
300 g/11 oz cooked long-grain rice
1 onion, finely chopped
100 g/4 oz mushrooms, sliced
beaten egg

Roll out the pastry thinly on a floured surface and cut out two equal-sized oblongs.

Combine the salmon with the butter, eggs, parsley and seasoning. Lay one oblong of pastry on a dampened baking tray. Spread half the rice on top, leaving a 1-cm/½-in border all round, and cover with the salmon, onion and mushrooms. Top with the remaining rice. Brush the edges of the pastry with beaten egg and lay the second pastry oblong over the mixture. Press the edges together firmly and pinch them up to look decorative. Make several slits with a sharp knife in the top and brush with beaten egg.

Place in a moderately hot oven (200 C, 400 F, gas 6) for 30–35 minutes, or until the pastry is well puffed and golden brown. Serve hot or cold.

JANSSON'S TEMPTATION

SERVES 4 TO 6

215 Kcals per portion

There are many stories about the origins of the name of this traditional Swedish dish. One common tale tells of Erik Jansson, a religious man – a self-made prophet or monk – who was opposed to all pleasures of the flesh, including the enjoyment of eating. However, when presented with this crisp and golden dish of potatoes, onions and anchovies he was overcome with temptation and took great pleasure in consuming the food.

75 g/3 oz butter
250 g/9 oz onions
1 kg/2 lb potatoes, thinly sliced
salt and pepper
1 (200-g) can tuna steak in oil
1 (50-g) can anchovies
250 ml/8 fl oz single cream
chopped parsley

Heat 25 g/1 oz of the butter in a frying pan. Add the onions and cook over a low heat for 5 minutes.

Grease an ovenproof dish with 25 g/1 oz of the butter and layer potatoes over the base. Add seasoning. Cover with the onions and tuna, including the oil. Arrange the remaining potatoes on top. Make a lattice pattern of the anchovy fillets over the top and pour over the can liquor. Dot with the remaining butter.

Place in a hot oven (220 C/425 F, gas 7) for 10 minutes and then pour over half the single cream. Cook for a further 15 minutes. Pour over the remaining cream and continue cooking for a further 30 minutes, or until the potato is soft and browned.

Serve hot, sprinkled with chopped parsley.

TUNA RISOTTO WITH NUTS

SERVES 4

590 Kcals per portion

Risottos – truly one-pan meals – can combine all sorts of ingredients with plenty of rice. The cooked risotto should be moist and full flavoured.

75 g/3 oz butter
1 tablespoon oil
1 small onion, finely chopped
1 garlic clove, crushed
250 g/9 oz long-grain rice
1 litre/1¾ pints fish or chicken stock
75 g/3 oz nuts, roughly chopped
(e.g. peanuts or walnuts)
50 g/2 oz dates, stoned and chopped
2 tablespoons sweetcorn
1 (200-g) can tuna steak in brine or oil,
drained
salt and pepper
chopped parsley

Heat the butter and oil in a heavy-based saucepan. Add the onion and garlic and cook gently until the onion is soft but not browned. Add the rice and continue to cook gently, stirring continuously, until the rice is slightly yellowed and shiny. Then add the stock. Take care not to burn your arm because the liquid will create a fierce puff of steam when it hits the hot oil.

Bring to the boil, stir lightly, reduce the heat, cover with a lid and simmer gently until the liquid has been absorbed – about 25 minutes. Add the nuts, dates, sweetcorn and tuna after 20 minutes. Give the mixture an occasional stir to prevent it drying out before the rice is cooked. Check the seasoning. Serve sprinkled with parsley.

◈ MICRO-TIP

Rice cooks very well in the microwave, saving slightly on time but mainly on washing up, since it can be cooked in the dish in which it is to be served.

Use a large dish to prevent boiling over during cooking. Cook the oil with the garlic and fat for 3 minutes on full power, then add boiling stock and the rice. Cover and cook on full power for 15–20 minutes. Add the remaining ingredients and cook for a further 5–7 minutes.

PAELLA

SERVES 6

350 Kcals per portion
(Illustrated on page 63)

A firm international favourite that needs no introduction, made with canned fish paella becomes a good store-cupboard standby. You can vary the canned fish you add – try adding baby clams if you like. The recipe calls for saffron, an authentic, expensive, ingredient. If you have saffron strands, then pound a few in a pestle and mortar to reduce them to a powder that will dissolve. For everyday cooking substitute ½ teaspoon turmeric.

1 (200-g) can tuna steaks in oil
1 (105-g) can smoked mussels
1 large onion, finely chopped
250 g / 9 oz tomatoes, peeled and chopped
1 teaspoon paprika
2 garlic cloves, crushed
salt and pepper
350 g / 12 oz long-grain rice
(use risotto rice if available)
1 litre / 1¾ pints fish stock
generous pinch of powdered saffron
100 g / 4 oz frozen peas
1 (100-g) can prawns, drained
1 (100-g) can shrimps, drained

Drain the tuna and mussels, and reserve the oil. Heat 2 tablespoons of the reserved oil in a frying pan. Add the onion and cook until soft but not browned. Add the tomatoes, paprika, garlic and seasoning. Cook gently for 5 minutes. Push the mixture to one side of the pan and fry the rice lightly in the oil. Add the stock, bring to the boil and add the saffron. Simmer, uncovered, for 15 minutes. Add all the remaining ingredients and stir them gently through the rice. Leave the pan over a low heat for 5 minutes before serving.

COOK'S TIP

All canned fish provides an excellent supply of easily digested protein that is necessary for everyone's good health, particularly growing children.

KEDGEREE

SERVES 4

375 Kcals per portion

Kedgeree is one of those well-known dishes that has interesting origins. Originally a spicy Indian dish combining rice and lentils, it was introduced to Britain and adapted to include fish.

1 (110-g) can sild in oil
1 onion, chopped
175 g / 6 oz long-grain rice
½ teaspoon turmeric
300 ml / ½ pint water
salt and pepper
2 hard-boiled eggs, chopped
50 g / 2 oz butter
2 tablespoons chopped parsley
2 tablespoons single cream

Drain the oil from the sild and heat it in a saucepan. Add the onion and cook until soft but not browned. Stir in the rice and turmeric, then pour in the water and add a little salt. Bring to the boil, cover the pan and reduce the heat. Simmer for 15–20 minutes, or until most of the liquid has been absorbed to leave the rice just moist.

Add the flaked sild, eggs and butter, forking these ingredients lightly into the rice. Cover closely with a lid or cooking foil and cook very gently for a further 10 minutes. Lightly fork in the parsley and cream, then check the seasoning before serving.

◈ MICRO-TIP

To cook the kedgeree in a microwave oven, place the oil and onion in a casserole dish and cook on full power for 3 minutes. Continue as above, cooking the rice, covered, on full power for 15 minutes. Add the remaining ingredients and cook for a further 5–7 minutes. Leave to stand for 3–5 minutes before serving.

CURRY

SERVES 4

100 Kcals per portion

The quality of this curry sauce depends on the curry powder you use – select a good quality powder for best results. If you have a good store of spices you may like to mix your own curry powder – follow the Cook's Tip for guidance. Once you have made the sauce, you can add a variety of canned fish. For example try adding pilchards and sardines in tomato sauce or brine, mackerel in brine, or tuna in oil or brine. The brine and tomato sauce can be added to the curry.

25 g/ I oz butter
I medium onion, chopped
I small cooking apple, cored, peeled and diced
2 tablespoons curry powder
25 g/ I oz plain flour
I garlic clove, crushed
$\frac{1}{2}$ teaspoon ground allspice
$\frac{1}{2}$ teaspoon ground coriander
I tablespoon tomato purée
I teaspoon curry paste
I tablespoon desiccated coconut
750 ml/ I$\frac{1}{4}$ pints stock
salt and pepper

Heat the butter in a frying pan. Add the onion and apple, and cook until soft but not browned. Stir in the curry powder and cook for I minute. Then add the flour and cook for a further minute. Add the garlic, spices, tomato purée, curry paste and coconut. Blend in the stock, bring to the boil and simmer for 15 minutes. Check the seasoning.

COOK'S TIP

You may like to grind you own spices for curry powder. Try 2 tablespoons coriander seeds with I tablespoon cumin seeds, I cinnamon stick, I teaspoon mustard seeds and 2 whole cardamom pods. Lightly roast the spices in a dry pan over a moderate heat, then cool slightly before grinding them to a powder in a pestle and mortar or coffee grinder. Add a good pinch of ground turmeric and chilli powder and mix well.

BIRIANI

SERVES 4

470 Kcals per portion

A biriani is the Indian equivalent of risotto – spices and rice are cooked with a variety of ingredients to produce a full-flavoured dish. You will find that canned sardines and mackerel both lend themselves very well to use in spicy recipes. If you have a small Indian or oriental shop near, then you may be able to buy fresh coriander leaves to chop and use instead of parsley on this biriani.

375 g/ 13 oz split red lentils
2 (120-g) cans sardines in oil
I large tomato, chopped
$\frac{1}{2}$ teaspoon ground cinnamon
I teaspoon chilli powder
2 cardamom seeds
I clove, crushed
3 black peppercorns, crushed
$\frac{1}{2}$ teaspoon turmeric
$\frac{1}{2}$ teaspoon ground cumin
$\frac{1}{2}$ teaspoon ground ginger
I onion, sliced
150 g/ 5 oz long-grain rice
4 small potatoes, sliced
300 ml/ $\frac{1}{2}$ pint fish or chicken stock
chopped parsley

Put the lentils into a saucepan, cover with water and bring to the boil. Boil for 10 minutes, then reduce the heat and simmer for 15–20 minutes. Drain thoroughly.

Drain the sardines and reserve the oil. Flake the fish with the tomato and spices. Heat the reserved oil from the sardines in a frying pan. Add the onion and cook until it is soft but not browned. Cook the rice in boiling water for 5 minutes and then drain.

Put 2 tablespoons of the oil in which the onion was fried into a saucepan. Add half the lentils, then the fish mixture and remaining lentils. Add half the rice, then the potatoes and remaining rice. Pour over the stock, cover and simmer for I hour.

Serve sprinkled with parsley.

LET'S GET TOGETHER

For most people having friends round for a meal is an informal affair when everyone can relax and share a bottle of wine and some food. Apart from inviting guests to an evening meal, why not gather people together for Sunday lunch or even brunch? Brunch is a late morning meal that makes up for missing breakfast and encompasses lunch – great for weekends. In the summer, if the weather warrants it then take to the garden and eat out of doors. In this chapter you will find ideas for canapés and dips which are perfect if you are planning a barbecue – offer them round while the coals are getting hot.

Remember that entertaining should be an enjoyable task – if you relax and feel at ease then the chances are your guests will do the same.

PRAWN COCKTAIL

SERVES 4

200 Kcals per portion

Shrimps can also be used to make these cocktails.

2 (200-g) cans prawns, drained
2 spring onions, trimmed and finely chopped
I small lettuce, trimmed and shredded
Dressing
150 ml/$\frac{1}{4}$ pint mayonnaise
I tablespoon tomato purée
Worcestershire sauce · salt and pepper
I tablespoon lemon juice
Garnish
lemon · chopped parsley

Mix the prawns with the spring onions. Divide the lettuce between four glass dishes. Mix the dressing ingredients, then stir in the prawns. Spoon into the glasses, garnish and serve.

TUNA COCKTAIL

SERVES 4 TO 6

100 Kcals per portion

I (185-g) can tuna chunks in oil
I (285-g) can peach slices in fruit juice
I tablespoon wine vinegar or cider vinegar
2 tablespoons natural yogurt
salt and pepper · 6 small gherkins
100 g/4 oz bean sprouts

Drain the tuna and reserve the oil. Drain the peaches and reserve the juice. Whisk I tablespoon of the reserved tuna oil with 2 tablespoons of the reserved peach juice and the vinegar. Mix in the yogurt and seasoning. Toss the tuna, cut-up peaches and sliced gherkins in the dressing.

Divide the bean sprouts between individual glasses and pile the tuna mixture on top.

Left: Fish Pâté Snacks (page 69) and Oysters en Brochette (page 72)

CRUDITÉS AND DIPS

Raw vegetables cut into neat, bite-size pieces or sticks, are known as crudités and they are a popular alternative to crisps and biscuits at parties.

Allow about 75 g/3 oz of crudités per portion. Cut celery, carrots, cucumber, and red and green peppers into small sticks. Cauliflower florets and button mushrooms can also be used.

SALMON DIP

SERVES 6

90 Kcals per portion

| 1 (213-g) can pink salmon, drained |
| 225 g/8 oz cottage cheese with chives |
| 1 tablespoon tomato ketchup |
| 2 teaspoons Worcestershire sauce |
| salt and pepper (optional) |

Blend all the ingredients together in a liquidiser. Alternatively use a fork to mash the ingredients thoroughly. Season with salt and pepper if necessary. Put the dip into a serving bowl and chill in a refrigerator before serving.

ZESTY FISH DIP

SERVES 6

80 Kcals per portion

| 2 (106-g) cans skippers in tomato sauce |
| 1 garlic clove, crushed (optional) |
| 6 tablespoons natural yogurt |
| $\frac{1}{2}$ cucumber, finely diced |
| 2 tablespoons tomato ketchup |

Mash the skippers and the sauce from the can with the garlic (if used), then stir in the yogurt and cucumber. Season with the tomato ketchup. Put the dip into a serving bowl and chill in the refrigerator before serving.

CRAB DIP À LA REINE

SERVES 8 TO 10

80 Kcals per portion

| 1 (170-g) can white meat crab, drained and flaked |
| 100 g/4 oz celery, finely chopped |
| 2 hard-boiled eggs, finely chopped |
| 2 tablespoons finely chopped onion |
| 200 ml/7 fl oz mayonnaise |
| grated nutmeg |
| lemon juice |
| salt and pepper |

Combine the crab with the celery, eggs, onion and mayonnaise. Season generously with nutmeg, lemon juice, salt and pepper, and mix well. Put the dip into a serving bowl and chill in a refrigerator before serving.

SKIPPER AND WALNUT BITES

SERVES 6

250 Kcals per portion

| 1 (106-g) can skippers in oil, drained |
| 175 g/6 oz cream cheese |
| 2 teaspoons lemon juice |
| 1 tablespoon chopped parsley |
| 100 g/4 oz shelled walnuts, crushed |

Mash the skippers and blend with the cream cheese, lemon juice and parsley. Roll teaspoons of the mixture in the walnuts. Chill in the refrigerator until needed and serve each one with a cocktail stick.

FISH PÂTÉ SNACKS

(Illustrated on page 65)

A simple fish pâté can be used for a variety of different canapés. Try some of these ideas if you are preparing snacks for a party; alternatively serve a plate of colourful canapés instead of a first course.

The one important tip to remember is to make all the canapés look as attractive as possible. Once arranged on platters or dishes, they can be loosely covered and kept in the refrigerator for a few hours.

Celery Boats
Scrub and trim celery sticks, cutting them into 5-cm/2-in lengths. Fill with pâté, using either a small teaspoon or a piping bag fitted with a star nozzle. Add quartered lemon slices or parsley sprigs if you like.

Cucumber Rounds
Cut fairly thick slices of cucumber and top with swirls of piped pâté. Top with a black olive and parsley sprig.

Cracker Bites
Spread the pâté over small cocktail crackers. Top with a criss-cross of halved anchovy fillets. Add half a stuffed olive, a parsley sprig or a small square of red pepper.

Stuffed Eggs
Halve some hard-boiled eggs and mash the yolks with the pâté. Pipe or spoon the mixture into the egg whites and top with a sprinkling of paprika or some chopped parsley.

Stuffed Tomatoes
Scoop out some very small tomatoes (use cherry tomatoes if available) and fill with pâté. Add a sprig of dill or watercress.

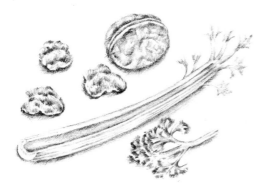

KIPPER PÂTÉ

SERVES 4

175 Kcals per portion

1 (200-g) can kipper fillets, drained
1 tablespoon soured cream
2 hard-boiled eggs, finely chopped
1 teaspoon chopped parsley
salt and pepper

Blend all the ingredients in a liquidiser or mash until smooth. Chill before serving.

Variation Use this recipe as a basis for making smoked mackerel pâté. Use smoked mackerel fillets and add a little grated lemon rind if you like.

SALMON AND DILL PÂTÉ

SERVES 6

210 Kcals per portion

100 g/4 oz butter or margarine, melted
1 (213-g) can pink salmon
50 g/2 oz cream cheese
25 g/1 oz fresh white breadcrumbs
1 teaspoon dill weed
a little Tabasco sauce or cayenne
salt and pepper
1 tablespoon lemon juice

Reserve half the butter or margarine. Blend or mash all the remaining ingredients until smooth. Put the pâté into a serving bowl and top with the reserved melted butter. Chill before serving.

SALMON MOUSSE

SERVES 4

280 Kcals per portion

25 g / 1 oz butter
25 g / 1 oz flour
250 ml / 8 fl oz milk
salt and pepper
1 tablespoon tomato purée
2 tablespoons water
15 g / ½ oz gelatine
1 (213-g) can pink salmon, drained and flaked
1 celery stick, finely chopped
2 tablespoons mayonnaise
4 tablespoons sherry
7 tablespoons double cream, whipped
Garnish
watercress or curly endive
sliced cucumber

Melt the butter in a saucepan, add the flour and blend in the milk gradually. Bring to the boil and cook, stirring continuously, until the sauce has thickened. Remove from the heat. Add seasoning and the tomato purée.

Heat the water until just boiling, then remove from the heat and add the gelatine. Stir until dissolved. Add to the sauce and leave to cool. Then add the salmon, celery, mayonnaise and sherry. When the mixture is nearly set, fold in the cream. Pour into a 1.15-litre/2-pint ring mould and chill in a refrigerator until set. Turn out on to a serving dish and garnish with watercress or endive and cucumber.

Variation Smoked mackerel mousse has a fuller flavour than salmon mousse but it can be made following the above recipe. Use smoked mackerel fillets and add the grated rind of 1 lemon together with a squeeze of lemon juice to the mixture.

COOK'S TIP

Mash soft cod roe with a squeeze of lemon juice, chopped parsley and pepper, then spread on hot buttered toast and brown under the grill.

SPINACH AND MACKEREL MOULD

SERVES 6

200 Kcals per portion

450 g| 1 lb large spinach leaves

1 (425-g) can mackerel steaks in brine

25 g| 1 oz butter

1 large onion, finely chopped

grated rind of 1 lemon

about 150 ml|$\frac{1}{4}$ pint fish stock

4 teaspoons gelatine

175 g| 6 oz sweetcorn, cooked

2 tomatoes, peeled, deseeded and chopped

salt and pepper

Garnish

lemon slices

tomato slices

Trim the stalks from the spinach leaves, then blanch them in boiling water for 2 minutes, drain and pat dry. Use to line a 1.15-litre/2-pint ring mould.

Drain the mackerel steaks and make up the liquid to 300 ml/$\frac{1}{2}$ pint with the stock. Melt the butter in a small pan. Add the onion and cook until soft not browned. Add the lemon rind; remove from the heat. Heat the liquid until just boiling, then remove from the heat and add the gelatine. Stir until dissolved.

Mash the fish, add to the onion and stir in the sweetcorn and tomatoes, adding seasoning to taste. When the liquid is beginning to set, stir it into the fish and pour into the mould. Chill until set.

To serve, turn the mould out on to a platter and cut into slices, then garnish as shown.

COOK'S TIP

Soft cod roe can be used to make a light, savoury fish mousse. Follow the main recipe, substituting 2 (100-g) cans soft cod roe for the salmon. Add 2 tablespoons chopped chives to the mixture.

CRAB BISQUE

SERVES 4

255 Kcals per portion

---

25 g / 1 oz butter

25 g / 1 oz flour

1 fish stock cube

750 ml / 1¼ pints boiling water

juice of ½ lemon

150 ml / ¼ pint dry white wine

1 (43-g) can dressed crab

salt and freshly ground black pepper

150 ml / ¼ pint double cream

chopped parsley

Melt the butter in a large saucepan over a low heat. Add the flour and stir to make a roux. Mix the stock cube with the boiling water and add to the roux, stirring continously. Add the lemon juice and wine. Whisk in the dressed crab. Season to taste and just before serving, stir in the cream. Sprinkle with chopped parsley and serve with crusty French bread or toast.

SWEET AND SAVOURY SKIPPER

SERVES 4

90 Kcals per portion

---

1 (106-g) can skippers in tomato sauce

4 tablespoons natural yogurt

1 teaspoon horseradish sauce

2 dessert apples, peeled, cored and diced

1 tablespoon chopped parsley

4 crisp lettuce leaves, shredded

1 red dessert apple, sliced and tossed in lemon juice

Use a fork to combine the skippers, yogurt, horseradish sauce, apple and parsley. Serve chilled on a bed of shredded lettuce, garnished with the red apple.

OYSTERS PARMESAN

SERVES 4

150 Kcals per portion

Canned smoked oysters are really worth discovering – they make any meal very special but they are not as extravagant as they sound! Combined with other ingredients they go a long way and give a good flavour.

---

15 g / ½ oz butter

15 g / ½ oz plain flour

300 ml / ½ pint milk

1 tablespoon grated Parmesan cheese

salt and pepper

1 (105-g) can smoked oysters, drained

25 g / 1 oz fine breadcrumbs

Melt the butter in a pan, stir in the flour and cook for 1–2 minutes. Remove from the heat and add the milk gradually. Bring to the boil slowly and simmer for 3 minutes, stirring continuously. Add the cheese and seasoning to taste. Put a few oysters in scallop shells or individual flameproof dishes and spoon over some of the cheese sauce. Top with breadcrumbs and place under a hot grill until the sauce bubbles and browns. Serve with Melba toast.

OYSTERS EN BROCHETTE

SERVES 6

105 Kcals per portion
(Illustrated on page 65)

---

1 (105-g) can smoked oysters, drained

150 g / 5 oz rindless bacon

Cut the bacon into 2.5-cm / 1-in pieces and roll up. Thread two bacon rolls on to a wooden cocktail stick with an oyster in between. Place the brochettes under a hot grill until the bacon is cooked.

CRAB MANDARIN APPETISER

SERVES 4

125 Kcals per portion

---

1 (298-g) can mandarin oranges in natural juice

½ honeydew melon, deseeded

lettuce leaves

1 (170-g) can white meat crab, drained

chopped parsley

Sauce

4 tablespoons mayonnaise

2 teaspoons Worcestershire sauce

1 teaspoon grated lemon rind

1 teaspoon tomato purée

salt and freshly ground black pepper

Drain the mandarin oranges, reserving the juice to drink or use in another recipe. Cut the melon flesh into balls with a melon baller. Tear the lettuce leaves into small pieces and put into a serving bowl. Combine the crab meat, mandarin oranges and melon. Blend the sauce ingredients together and mix lightly with the shellfish mixture. Pile on the bed of lettuce and chill in the refrigerator before serving sprinkled with parsley.

STUFFED MUSHROOMS

SERVES 4

210 Kcals per portion

---

4 large open mushrooms

2 (106-g) cans skippers in oil, drained

1 spring onion, finely diced

1 tablespoon fresh breadcrumbs

50 g/2 oz Cheddar cheese, grated

Wipe the mushrooms clean with a damp cloth. Mix all the remaining ingredients together; divide the mixture between the mushrooms and spread over the cup sides. Arrange on a baking tray, cover and cook in a moderately hot oven (200C, 400F, gas 6) for 15 minutes. Remove the covering and cook for a further 5 minutes.

Alternatively, place the stuffed mushrooms under a moderate grill for 10–15 minutes. Serve hot with crusty bread.

SALMON SCALLOPS

SERVES 4

250 Kcals per portion

These make a satisfying starter or they can be turned into an elegant dish for lunch or supper by piping a border of mashed potato round the shells or dishes. For a main course use 1 (400-g) can red salmon.

---

butter for dishes

3 tablespoons very fine breadcrumbs

1 (213-g) can red salmon

about 350 ml/12 fl oz milk

40 g/1½ oz butter

40 g/1½ oz flour

75 g/3 oz Cheddar cheese, grated

salt and pepper

Butter four scallop shells or individual flameproof dishes and coat with some of the breadcrumbs. Drain the salmon and reserve the oil. Divide the fish between the dishes, doming it higher in the centre.

Make up the reserved oil to 375 ml/13 fl oz with the milk. Melt the butter in a saucepan, stir in the flour and cook for 2–3 minutes. Remove the pan from the heat and stir in the milk mixture gradually. Bring to the boil and continue to stir until the sauce thickens. Add 50 g/2 oz of the cheese and seasoning. Pour the sauce over the salmon. Sprinkle with the remaining breadcrumbs and cheese. Place under a moderate grill for a few minutes to brown.

SALMON SALAD PLATTER

SERVES 4

370 Kcals per portion

1 (440-g) can red salmon, drained
4 large lettuce leaves
4 hard-boiled eggs
1 (43-g) can dressed crab
lemon juice · salt and pepper
6 tablespoons mayonnaise
1 (340-g) can asparagus spears, drained
½ cucumber, peeled and chopped
1 tablespoon chopped chives
8 small squares brown bread, buttered

Divide the salmon into four portions and remove the bones. Arrange the lettuce down the centre of a large platter and put a portion of salmon on each.

Halve the eggs, remove the yolks and press through a sieve. Reserve some of the yolk for garnish. Mix the remainder with the crab, lemon juice and seasoning. Pipe or spoon the mixture into the egg whites and arrange around the salmon. Spoon some of the mayonnaise on top of the salmon and eggs and sprinkle with the reserved egg yolk.

Cut about 2.5 cm/1 in from the tips of the asparagus spears and use to garnish the salmon. Cut up the remaining asparagus and mix with the cucumber, chives, remaining mayonnaise and seasoning. Pile on to the bread squares and place between the eggs.

COOK'S TIP

Making Melba Toast

Take 4 medium thick slices of bread and toast lightly on both sides. Working quickly before the toast cools and becomes too crisp, cut off the crusts and slice through each piece of toast to give very thin pieces. Brown the uncooked sides under a moderately hot grill, keeping the toast away from the grill so that it has plenty of room to curl. Cool on a wire rack. The cooled toast can be stored for a couple of weeks in an airtight tin.

Using the same technique you can make very small squares of the toast and serve them with dips as snacks.

SALADE NIÇOISE

SERVES 4

230 Kcals per portion

This traditional recipe makes an excellent first course – divide the salad between individual plates or glass dishes and serve with crunchy bread or crisp Melba toast. Tuna can be used instead of the salmon.

1 (213-g) can red salmon, drained
1 lettuce
4 potatoes, cooked and diced
100 g/ 4 oz green beans, cooked
1 (50-g) can anchovy fillets, drained
12 black olives
4 tomatoes, quartered
2 hard-boiled eggs, quartered
4 tablespoons mayonnaise

Flake the salmon coarsely. Arrange the lettuce leaves in a salad bowl. Cover with the potatoes, then the green beans and the salmon. Garnish with the anchovies, olives, tomatoes and hard-boiled eggs. Spoon the mayonnaise over the salad.

TUNA FONDUE

SERVES 4 TO 6

425 Kcals per portion

1 garlic clove, halved
250 ml/ 8 fl oz dry cider
1 teaspoon lemon juice
500 g/ 18 oz Cheddar cheese, grated
1 tablespoon cornflour
25 g/ 1 oz butter
black pepper
2 tablespoons Worcestershire sauce
2 tablespoons dry sherry
1 (185-g) can tuna chunks in brine, drained and flaked

Rub the inside of a ceramic fondue pan with the cut garlic; discard the garlic. Add the cider and lemon juice, and heat gently. Mix together the cheese, cornflour and butter. Add the mixture gradually to the cider. Season with pepper. Cook over a low heat, stirring continuously, until the cheese has melted and the mixture is creamy. Stir in the Worcestershire sauce, sherry and tuna. Serve with cubes of French bread, cucumber and celery.

LUXURY SEAFOOD QUICHE

SERVES 6

410 Kcals per portion

This delicious quiche is made extra special by the pastry base which is a cream cheese dough. The quiche can be served hot or cold.

Cream Cheese Pastry
I egg yolk
2 teaspoons water
175 g/6 oz plain flour
pinch of salt
pinch of paprika
100 g/4 oz cream cheese
50 g/2 oz butter, softened
Filling
25 g/1 oz butter
I medium green pepper, deseeded and sliced
50 g/2 oz button mushrooms, wiped and sliced
3 eggs
7 tablespoons milk
7 tablespoons single cream
salt and pepper
I garlic clove, crushed
I (125-g) can mackerel fillets in oil, drained
I (105-g) can smoked mussels, drained
I (100-g) can shrimps, rinsed and drained

Beat the egg yolk and water until well blended. Sift together the flour, salt and paprika into a basin. Add the remaining pastry ingredients and mix together to form a soft manageable dough. Roll out on a floured board to 5-mm/¼-in thickness and use to line a 28-cm/11-in oval ovenproof flan dish. Prick the base of the pastry and bake blind in a moderately hot oven (200C, 400F, gas 6) for 10 minutes.

Meanwhile melt the butter in a frying pan and cook the green pepper and mushrooms. Whip together the eggs, milk, cream and seasoning. Arrange the vegetable mixture, garlic and fish in the base of the flan. Pour over the egg mixture and bake for a further 25 minutes or until set.

SALMON AND MUSHROOM QUICHE

SERVES 4

430 Kcals per portion

175 g/6 oz plain flour
pinch of salt
75 g/3 oz butter
about 4 tablespoons water
Filling
I (213-g) can pink salmon, drained and flaked
100 g/4 oz button mushrooms, sliced
2 eggs
250 ml/8 fl oz milk
100 g/4 oz Edam cheese, grated
salt and pepper

Sift the flour and salt into a basin. Rub in the butter until the mixture resembles breadcrumbs. Add sufficient water to make a firm dough. Roll out on a floured board to 5-mm/¼-in thickness and use to line an 18-cm/7-in flan ring.

Put the salmon and mushrooms in the pastry case. Mix together the eggs, milk, cheese and seasoning, then pour over the salmon. Place in a hot oven (220C, 425F, gas 7) for 25–30 minutes, or until the filling is set.

COOK'S TIP

For a very special starter, prepare individual quiches. Make them in six individual quiche dishes measuring about 7.5-cm/3-in. in diameter.

TUNA CURRY VOL-AU-VENT

SERVES 4

640 Kcals per portion

You can always cheat and buy a prepared frozen vol-au-vent case.

375 g/13 oz puff pastry
1 (185-g) can tuna chunks in oil
1 tablespoon curry powder
2 teaspoons flour
2 teaspoons curry paste
grated rind and juice of 1 lemon
2 tablespoons desiccated coconut, infused in
300 ml/$\frac{1}{2}$ pint boiling water
1 cooking apple, peeled, cored and diced
1 tablespoon mango chutney
2 tablespoons sweetcorn
salt and pepper

Roll out the puff pastry into a circle measuring slightly larger than 20-cm/8-in. Invert a 20-cm/8-in plate over the pastry and use the tip of a sharp knife to cut round. Remove the plate and use the tip of the knife to mark an inner circle, leaving a 1-cm/$\frac{1}{2}$-in border and being careful not to cut right through the pastry. Place the pastry circle on a damp baking tray and cook in a hot oven (220 C, 425 F, gas 7) for 20 minutes, or until golden brown. Use a sharp knife to loosen the inner circle and then lift this off.

Drain the oil from the fish into a saucepan and heat gently. Blend in the curry powder, flour and curry paste, and cook for 2–3 minutes. Add the grated lemon rind and juice, coconut stock, apple and mango chutney; simmer for 20 minutes. Stir in the sweetcorn and tuna; check the seasoning. Bring to the boil and then turn into the hot vol-au-vent case. Top with the inner pastry circle.

KIPPER AND APPLE PATTIES

MAKES 12 TO 14

275 Kcals per portion

225 g/8 oz shortcrust pastry
7 tablespoons white sauce
1 (200-g) can kipper fillets, drained and diced
2 red dessert apples, cored and chopped
generous pinch of dried dill weed
salt and pepper
lemon juice
finely chopped parsley

Roll out the pastry on a floured board to 5-mm/$\frac{1}{4}$-in thickness and use to line 12–14 shallow patty tins. Chill for 30 minutes, prick the pastry all over, then bake in a moderately hot oven (190 C, 375 F, gas 5) for 10–15 minutes or until firm and golden. Cool.

Mix the white sauce with the kippers, apple, herb, seasoning and lemon juice to taste. Divide between the pastry cases. Sprinkle with parsley.

COOK'S TIP

Making a Vol-au-vent Case
1 Cut out the pastry circle.
2 Use the point of a knife to mark the inner circle, leaving 1-cm/$\frac{1}{2}$-in border, without cutting right through the pastry.
3 Carefully loosen and lift off the inner circle when cooked.

TUNA CREOLE

SERVES 4

300 Kcals per portion

1 tablespoon oil
1 onion, finely chopped
1 green pepper, deseeded and diced
1 green chilli, deseeded and chopped (optional)
1 celery stick, diced
1 tablespoon plain flour
1 (397-g) can tomatoes
1 teaspoon mixed herbs
2 teaspoons lemon juice
salt and pepper
Worcestershire sauce (optional)
2 (185-g) cans tuna chunks in brine, drained
225 g/8 oz long-grain rice
300 ml/½ pint water

Heat the oil in a frying pan. Add the onion, green pepper, chilli (if used) and celery, and cook over a low heat until soft but not browned. Stir in the flour and cook for 2 minutes. Add the tomatoes, herbs, lemon juice, seasoning and a dash of Worcestershire sauce (if used). Bring to the boil, then cover and simmer for 10 minutes. Add the drained tuna and cook gently without stirring for 5 minutes.

Meanwhile put the rice in a saucepan and add a little salt. Pour in the water and bring to the boil. Cover the pan, reduce the heat and simmer for about 20 minutes, or until the grains are tender and the water has been absorbed.

Divide the rice between four plates and top with the tuna sauce. Serve at once.

◈ MICRO-TIP

To cook the Tuna Creole in the microwave, place the vegetables and oil in a casserole dish and cook for 5–6 minutes. Add the other ingredients, as above, cover and cook for 5–7 minutes.

Cook the rice in a large dish, covered, for 15–20 minutes, until the liquid has been absorbed.

YOU ARE WHAT YOU EAT

The importance of good diet in achieving good health is one that we are all aware of. The chart below gives a nutritional breakdown of John West canned fish – it is useful when planning your diet.

A Balanced Diet   Remember to include variety in your diet. 'Eat your meat, it's good for you' is now rather an out-of-date phrase with the emphasis being on reducing the overall intake of meat to leave room for more fish and vegetables. Canned fish provides all the goodness found in fresh fish with the great advantages of having no bones and needing little or no preparation. You will find that canned fish is an ideal food to introduce into a youngster's diet – they like the flavour of the milder fish, like tuna or salmon, and they are safe to eat the fish without having to pick out bones.

Take stock of the fat and sugar contents of your diet – are you over-indulging in these foods? If so, then make an effort to reduce the overall intake of both, using skimmed milk and low-fat cheeses if you really are cutting down on the fatty foods.

Make sure you are getting enough fibre. This is provided by brown rice and pulses, wholemeal bread or pastry, cereals and unpeeled vegetables.

Exercise and Relaxation   Exercise and relaxation are closely related and they both work hand in hand with diet when it comes to good health. You do not have to spend hours running or taking vigorous sport to keep healthy. Simply walk regularly, increasing the distance as you feel fitter.

Relaxing is all about getting rid of the everyday worries and slowing down for a short while each day. How you achieve this is best for you to decide – some people have a hobby, others prefer to do a few simple floor exercises. Whatever you do, if you end up feeling calm and in control when you have finished, then you are achieving the aim.

Before you embark on any diet or exercise programme, remember to consult your doctor first to make sure that you are fit and healthy.

NUTRITIONAL INFORMATION
Contents (in grammes) are average per 100 g/4 oz fish

Product	Cals	Fat	Protein
RED SALMON	210	15	18.7
MEDIUM RED SALMON	167	10.1	19
PINK SALMON	140	6.8	19.6
KETA SALMON	121	4	20
TUNA *in oil (drained)*	197	10.6	26.3
TUNA *in brine (drained)*	110	0.65	26
SANDWICH TUNA *in oil*	296	26	16.2
SANDWICH TUNA *in brine*	93	1.1	20.5
SARDINES *in oil (drained)*	197	11.8	22.9
SARDINES *in brine*	170	20	8
SARDINES *in tomato sauce*	176	11.6	17
SILD *in oil (drained)*	227	16.3	19.7
SILD *in tomato sauce*	172	9.7	20.6
KIPPER FILLETS	228	15.9	21.3
HERRING FILLETS *in savoury sauce*	118	5.6	13.2

Product	Cals	Fat	Protein
HERRING FILLETS *in tomato sauce*	138	7.9	14.5
MACKEREL *in tomato sauce*	290	25	16.5
MACKEREL *in brine*	200	12	22.0
SMOKED MACKEREL *in oil (drained)*	314	25.1	22.2
PRESSED COD ROES	104	3.6	15.8
SOFT COD ROES	66	12	2
PILCHARDS *in brine*	150	6.0	24.0
SHRIMPS	91	1.1	20.3
PRAWNS	86	1.2	18.8
SKIPPERS *in oil*	293	23.3	20.8
SKIPPERS *in tomato*	154	9.5	16.5
DRESSED CRAB	138	6.7	16.7

Note: Dressed crab also contains 3 g carbohydrate per 100 g/4 oz

RECIPE INDEX